Mothers
NEVER DIE

Beverly Rose

Mothers NEVER DIE

BEVERLY ROSE

INTEGRITY®
PUBLISHERS
Nashville

MOTHERS NEVER DIE

Published in association with the literary agency of Alive Communications, Inc., 7680 Goddard Street, Suite 200, Colorado Springs, CO 80920.

Cover Design: Bill Chiaravalle, Sisters, OR
Interior Design: PerfecType, Nashville, TN

ISBN 1-59145-016-0

Printed in the United States of America
02 03 04 05 06 BVG 9 8 7 6 5 4 3 2 1

This book
is dedicated
to my mother—

who imparted to me a tradition
of wisdom, ethics, and justice,
rooted in *selfless* love and faith,
inspiring me to rise to a
new life of humility and grace.

CONTENTS

Prologue

She would have liked him if she had known him. They had so much in common. She practiced love. He preached it. She saw the virtue in everyone. He sat with outcasts and sinners. She performed good deeds. He gave selflessly to all. She was admirable and God-fearing. He was praiseworthy and faithful. She was born Jewish. So was he.

Yet she believed him to be a fraud, an instigator responsible for the murder of millions who were slaughtered in his name. She even blamed him for the annihilation of most of her family. Just the mention of his name sent chills down her spine and resentment echoing through her soul. It was a name of pain that caused in her the greatest despair—and made being Jewish all the harder.

She was my mother.

And he . . . he claimed the name above all names.

PART 1

Mother

ON MY MIND

The LORD is close to the brokenhearted. . . .

PSALM 34:18

1

I SAW HER DIE . . .
Twice

April 2, 1998

She's dead. That's no exaggeration. I saw her die . . . twice. Once in March. Once in April. The first time was on a Saturday morning in spring. Under a breathtaking blue sky, as the gentle Floridian breezes ushered in the beginnings of new life, she lay gasping for air. Forcing herself from bed, she staggered to my room, jolting me from a sound sleep. "I don't feel well." That was all she said. She just about made it back to bed before she collapsed.

"Hello, 911? My mother—she's barely breathing. How soon can you get here?"

"As soon as we can, ma'am." Soon wasn't soon enough.

"Mom, breathe!" I begged her lifeless body. Her chest rose and fell, expelling one precious breath in a thundering snort. I sighed with relief. She fell silent.

"Mom, breathe!" I yelled, commanding her to live . . . another rise and fall . . . then nothing. I gasped . . . she didn't. I panicked. That's what you do when your mother drops dead right in front of you on a Saturday morning in spring. I forgot everything I ever learned about CPR and regressed to the age of two.

"Mom, I love you, I love you!" I shouted louder and louder. But she wasn't deaf . . . just dead. She didn't budge. Her muscles went stiff. Her eyes became fixed and glassy. She looked like a piece of furniture, an accessory to the bedroom set she had purchased as a newlywed nearly forty-one years earlier.

"Hello, 911? I called before. My mother—"

"Yeah, we know, we know. We're coming."

"So is Godot," I muttered under my breath.

I returned to the inanimate object that was my mother. Finally an insight—I breathed into her frozen mouth. She stirred. Her eyes morphed into agents of sight. Her muscles softened and relaxed. Reverse rigor mortis. She spoke.

"I was floating. It was so nice and peaceful. Then I heard you say 'I love you,' and I decided to come back."

From the dead, Mom?

But she never knew she was dead . . . just somewhere better than this.

She wasn't back for long, though. The paramedics finally arrived and carted her away. The medical system prodded and punctured her and, ultimately, lost her. "Complications after open-heart surgery," they explained when there was no explanation. She had been given a 98 percent chance of survival. She was in the 2 percent.

My brother and I were there when she died again. It was grotesque. Tubes protruded from every orifice of her swollen, twitching body. Monitors kept the deathwatch, numbers gravely sinking downward. My brother and I chanted again and again at her bedside: "Shema Yisrael Adonai Elohenu Adonai Echad" ("Hear, O Israel, the Lord is our God, the Lord is One"). She may have heard our gut-wrenching prayers as we cried out these most sacred words in Judaism. But this time she did not come back.

Jews light memorial candles every year in remembrance of the lives of the dearly departed. I end up remembering the death I wish I could forget. "Yit-gadal v'yit-kadash sh'may raba. . . ." For eleven years, I have faithfully said the Mourner's Prayer over the tiny candle, but I'm sure I never get it right. The garbled prayer releases itself in spits and sputters, hardly resembling its mother tongue. I worry that I might be inadvertently stumbling upon unintended phrases. Am I really saying, "Attention K-Mart shoppers, today's blue-light special is . . ."?

It's absurd how I struggle to speak Hebrew in honor of my dead mother. I never learned the language. My father gave me a choice— clarinet lessons or Hebrew school. Let's just say I play a mean "Hava Nagila." Perhaps I should belt out a chorus of this spirited song rather than struggle with unpronounceable prayers. It might be a more fitting tribute. My mother always loved my performances with Dad at temple gatherings and nursing homes . . . that is, before I became so disabled that my beloved instruments fell silent more than a decade ago. "And here's a little tune I'm sure you folks all know. Mom, this one's for you."

The show must go on. It is dark in the failing light of sunset. It is time. The memorial candle awaits its mission. It will burn for twenty-four hours, from sunset to sunset, on the Hebrew calendar date that marks the anniversary of her death. I fumble for a match. My weak fingers barely budge. I nudge the lethargic appendages. "Come on! The sun will set before this darn candle will be lit, and then it will be too late." Too late for what? She's been dead for years. I struggle to grasp. I fail. My stronger left hand snatches the matchbox, having been partially spared the ravages of this illness . . . for now.

Unceremoniously, I place a small, frayed terry-cloth towel on my head. My mother would have donned a special head covering for this solemn occasion. That's what observant Jews do. But not I, I observe. The match strikes the flint, and a tiny flicker pierces the darkness, I guide the fledgling flame toward the candle. Flirting with the wick, the dancing light gives of itself, sparking new birth. The heat of ignition sears my fingertips. I vigorously shake the match flame out of existence. It has given life. Now it must be extinguished . . . but not forgotten.

Shadows suddenly pulsate with light as flickering memories invade my mind—reruns of old horrors, death scenes to be relived again and again. Not by her . . . but by me. She has mercifully escaped these dreaded images. A person who dies has a chance to become heir to new life. But we, in life, are certain to inherit their death.

Why, God? Why did you take her from me? I know you are a loving God. So why did she die when she was so vibrant and had so much to live for? Only twelve years in retirement—a small consolation after a lifetime of hardship. It wasn't her fault that she grew up in dire poverty and had no winter coat during those harsh New York City winters in the 1920s. Couldn't you protect that poor nine-year-old child from the bone-chilling cold and the rheumatic fever that ravaged her body and damaged her heart? Were you there to comfort her as she watched the other children learn to ride bicycles and play hopscotch while she was confined to bed for all those years? Is it fair that she was left with a dysfunctional heart valve that plagued her all her life? Is there a reason why she died trying to have it replaced with a pig valve?

"Such an unkosher alternative! Maybe I should choose the synthetic one!" she had said, smiling. What warmth and humor she could muster, even in the most dire circumstances.

A chill seizes my body. The room is stone cold and deadly silent. Jennifer stirs from her reveries and stares at me just long enough to ascertain if it is time to eat again. Seeing that I serve no useful purpose for her at the moment, she buries her head in the blanket and resumes her nap. I envy her blissful ignorance of life's trials. This loving canine, my constant companion for more than a decade, is unaware of the tragic circumstances of my existence. She cares not that the hands that caress and feed her grow weak and tremulous. Nor does it matter to her that I have lost so much in my life since her adoption.

I remember proudly walking out of the pet shop with my new furry family member. It was only thirteen years ago . . . yet it seems like a lifetime. I had a blossoming professional career as a clinical psychologist, an impressive salary, and a condo on a beautiful New England lake west of Boston. Finally all my dreams were coming true. Yet it was becoming increasingly difficult to ignore the fatigue and muscle pain that were overtaking my body. I struggled to push through the symptoms, hoping they would eventually subside. I was never one to coddle myself. I had neither the time nor the inclination to rest—not after surviving the rigors of a postdoctoral year at a Harvard-affiliated teaching hospital, accepting a staff appointment, and then rising to the position of associate director of a regional nursing-home program. I had worked my whole life for such prestige, financial security, and professional independence. It was all within my reach . . . but apparently not my grasp.

I stare down at the weakened right hand in repose on my lap. "Grasping has not come easily lately," I mutter. Nor can I grasp the enormity of what has happened to me. I survey the austere room, remembering my lakeside condo. My mind is flooded with images of

9

iridescent-feathered ducks floating aimlessly on the timeless ripples of sparkling water as Canada geese sail in the sky above. Dim streaks of candlelight mock my reverie, illuminating the spartan decor of government-subsidized housing. No amenities here. No spectacular New England views of exotic wildlife except for the occasional sighting of my neighbor across the way who resembles some kind of unusual mammal, as yet unclassified. But why should I single him out? Here we are all marginals of society, the disenfranchised living in a low-income housing project designed for the elderly and people with disabilities. *It's better that you are dead, Mom, than to have lived to see the depths to which my life has sunk.*

So that's it. I killed you! A flash of insight breaks through the dam of unanswered questions. *I broke your heart when, twelve years ago, I showed up so terribly ill at your doorstep in Florida with nothing but shattered dreams in my eyes. Did you feel helpless when all you could do was take me in and give me nurturance and shelter? Did you hear the voices of our ancestors crying out in agony as the dreams they carried with them across the ocean crashed against the rocks? Did you hear the wailing of your deceased parents, the courageous immigrants who escaped the pogroms in Russia, the death raids against Jews, so that their progeny would have a chance at a better life in this promised land?*

It was I who had achieved the first doctorate in the family and was awarded membership in the hallowed halls of the Ivy League. "From shtetl to superstar!" I proclaim bitterly to no one listening. Life had finally made reparations for generations of struggle and hardship. Finally justice, even vindication, so painstakingly achieved, so quickly and cruelly snatched. By whose hand?

I gasp for breath amid the waves of uncontrollable sobbing.

"Mom, if only you could hear me crying out to you in this awful, ago-nizing darkness."

The room remains painfully silent. My stomach grumbles. It is well past the dinner hour. A bitter taste lingers in my mouth, a mixture of unpalatable memories and salty tears. My aching body sinks into the thick foam cushion designed to shield my muscles from the pain of sit-ting. There is no shelter from the agony of life. My eyelids, wet and heavy from too many tears, close uneasily. I nod off in restless slumber . . .

> *"Beverly . . ."*
> *I stir.*
> *"Beverly, I can."*
> *Startled, I struggle to see. Goosebumps run up and down my spine. I can barely move.*
> *"What? What did you say?" I respond almost auto-matically to the hauntingly familiar voice.*
> *"I said, 'I can . . . I can hear you.'"*
> *"Mom, is that you?"*
> *"Were you speaking to someone else?" The loving warmth of the teasing voice is unmistakable.*
> *"No. But . . . I thought . . . I mean . . . you're dead."*
> *"In a manner of speaking, Beverly, but not really."*
> *"What do you mean, 'not really'? Either you are dead, or you are not dead."*
> *"Mothers never die when they are remembered in the hearts of their children."*
> *"Then we will be together forever, Mom."*
> *"Beverly, you were always so clever."*

"If only smarts were enough," I whisper under my breath. I feel strangely embarrassed meeting her again in the failed circumstances of my life. Yet I know she loves me unconditionally. She always has.

"Oy vey," she sighs deeply. "Why couldn't it have all worked out for you the way you wanted it to?"

Now I know this really is my mother. No one else can enunciate that well-worn Yiddish phrase as well as she can. Her timing is perfect, her intonation stirring, her inflection indisputably convincing. She has sculpted and refined her flawless delivery over countless years of suffering. It is her signature, a profound summation of life from a woman who has witnessed it all, perhaps having seen too much. If she were less humble, I would have had a vanity license plate fashioned especially for her. It would announce OY VEY . . . FLORIDA."

"I'm so sorry that I broke your heart, Mom."

"Don't say that, Beverly. You didn't break my heart. It wasn't your fault."

"Then why did you die, Mom, when I needed you so much?"

As she begins to answer with her favorite Yiddish expression, I jump in, proudly translating the familiar phrase into English. "I know, Mom: 'Man plans and God laughs.'"

"I'm pleased you still remember."

"I remember everything about you, Mom—the fragrance of your perfume, the subtle color of your blue-gray eyes, your precious wisdom, your brilliant sense of humor."

"I'm glad to see that you still love me so much, Beverly. But maybe it's too much. Maybe it's time to move on with your life, meet a nice Jewish boy, get married already." A second indisputable proof that this is indeed the voice of my dead mother. She would even return from the grave to remind me of this one more time.

"I know, Mom, I know. I want that more than anything in life. But things have not exactly been easy around here with this illness . . ." I am about to launch into a familiar mix of explanation and apology when I stop myself abruptly. *"Oh no, I have forgotten about . . . him!"*

"Who?" My mom's ears perk up at the mention of a pronoun in the masculine gender.

"Uh . . ." I pause to buy time, reflecting upon how to best answer this incredibly difficult question. *"Him . . . my . . . my . . . rabbi . . . sort of . . . friend."*

"Rabbi friend?" Her expectant voice rises. She can hardly contain herself. Luckily, she is out of body.

"Yes." The shock of such a revelation would ordinarily have killed her—that is, if she weren't already dead.

"Is he single? How old is he? Where did you meet him? Was he married before?" Apparently the long, eleven-year heavenly repose has not dulled her expert interrogatory skills.

"Well, Mom, that's a long story."

"I have plenty of time, Beverly."

13

"I know, Mom—an eternity. Hopefully, my story won't take that long."

Our eyes exchange playful glances as we embrace each other in a timeless dance of souls. It is as if we had never parted.

"So, who is this rabbi, Beverly? Please don't keep your poor Jewish mother in suspense!"

"Well, Mom, remember when I came to stay with you several months before you died? I was terribly ill and thought I could recuperate in Florida. Then you passed away unexpectedly, and I was left to battle this disabling illness while suffering the grief of losing you. Well, shortly after your death, I returned to Boston in hopes of finding a cure. When that failed, I spent several frustrating, unproductive years in intensive physical therapy in Arizona, hoping to recover my health in the dry, warm climate. Instead, my condition worsened. Returning to Boston, I lay in bed for years, wondering how I could possibly go on. I was convinced that I could no longer lead a meaningful and productive life . . . not after losing my health, along with almost everything else of importance. I felt horribly desperate and alone."

"That's terrible, Beverly. I am so sorry it has been so hard for you. If I could have been there, you know I would have."

"I know, Mom. But just when I was at my lowest ebb, when I thought I could not go on any longer, I met the rabbi. Miraculously, he changed everything for me."

"That's amazing, Beverly. Do you have a close relationship with him?"

"Very close, Mom. He is the reason I have a renewal of hope and joy. Through him, my life is filled with new meaning despite my suffering."

"He must be quite a man."

"And so much more."

"So, who is he? Where does he come from?"

"He's a gift from God."

"Apparently! But what is his name? What temple is he affiliated with? Of all the rabbis you have known, why is he the one who was able to make such a difference in your life?"

"That's a great question, Mom. Actually, I am thinking of writing a book about that."

"You are writing a book? How wonderful! I always said that you wrote so beautifully. Remember those lovely birthday cards you sent me? Not to mention all those English awards in school."

"Maybe you could even help me write it. I'm trying to decide how and where to begin my life story."

I pause, hoping she will not feel intimidated. She had always lamented not being able to afford to go to college. What a shame. She was one of the most intelligent people I have ever known.

She replies eagerly, "How about if you begin with your grandparents escaping the pogroms in Russia to come to America? To think my mother

*survived that terrible journey while pregnant with
me at the time!"*

"That would be a perfect place to begin, Mom."

*"I can't wait to hear about this rabbi of yours. He
sounds so mysterious, Beverly. Is he real or are you making him up just to please your old Jewish mother?"*

*I start to say, "You're not old, Mom . . . just dead,"
but think better of it. "Oh, he's very real, Mom."*

*"Then when can I meet him? Seeing is believing,
you know."*

*I ponder how to best answer this troubling question.
I fear she will fail to see what I see in him . . . and may
even cease to believe in me. "Well, Mom," I reply with
trepidation, "sometimes believing is seeing."*

What's that slobbering all over my hand? Such soft fur, a tongue
. . . I awaken abruptly. Focusing my eyes, I struggle to see. I can't
believe what a strange dream I had—my mother . . . revisited. The
moonlight filters through the blinds. I rub my tired eyes. What time
is it? I am afraid to look. I feel a tug at my hand. "Jennifer!" Have I
forsaken my maternal duties and neglected to feed my poor Shih Tzu
her dinner? I force my aching, complaining body from the chair to
attend to the realities of life. Or, should I say, to this present reality.

Still alive. The tiny flicker of the memorial candle dances in the still-
ness of morning. I strain to pry open my crusted eyelids. They resist,

pasted shut by too little sleep and too many tears. The glow of the flame appears pale and insignificant in the light of day. This little sparkler, which cast giant shadows in the murky darkness of yesterday's sunset, reveals itself in the light of morning to be but a tiny gleam in the eye of a vast universe. "Only nine hours to go," I blurt out. The petite flame flickers, skirting around the huge puff of air I have inadvertently blown in its direction. I marvel at its ability to withstand such a rude assault. The secret of its fragile existence seems to be: In a world filled with a lot of hot air, sway gracefully in the breeze. The rabbi would understand. He has elevated grace to an art form.

I rub my stiff muscles and rise. It has been a fitful night of painful limbs and disturbing thoughts ushered in by vivid memories of my mother's death—memories I will have to endure if I am to capture them in print. Sepia images of distant, foreign faces flash through my mind—relatives whom I never knew or barely knew captured in time in tattered photographs—ancestors who paved the golden road on which I walked . . . and stumbled.

I make my way to the kitchen and prepare a large portion of cereal, more out of habit than hunger. Pushing the brimming bowl aside, I ponder how best to begin my book. The morning meal will still be there when I have summoned the appetite. I have never gone hungry. Others in my family have not been so lucky. So I've been told . . .

PART 2

It's a Question

OF FAITH

And what does the LORD require of you?
To act justly and to love mercy
and to walk humbly with your God.

MICAH 6:8

MY GRANDPARENTS'
Great Escape

June 20, 1914

"Hurry up!" she shouts with impatience. He barely stirs. She eyes him with annoyance as she stuffs their few remaining possessions into the tattered sack. There is so little time. She reaches for the precious candlesticks high upon the shelf, being careful to cradle them gently in her callused hands. A tear escapes from her weary eye as she caresses the treasured relics. Sadly, such sacred holders of light can no longer brighten the dark recesses of an enslaved soul. Yet even in czarist Russia she has unwavering faith in God.

"Perhaps in the New World . . . ," she sighs deeply as she glances at her husband. He sits motionless, his vacant eyes staring past her into the bright future he will never see. He can hardly bear to watch her last-minute preparations. An agonizing pain of resignation courses through his trembling body. She forces herself back to the dreaded task at hand. "I'm telling you for the last time. Get up from that chair and gather your things. We will be late!" Her pleas fall on ears that refuse to hear any more. "If you don't get up right now, I am going to leave without you. I mean it. I'll go all the way to America by myself if I have to. At least I'll live to see the rest of my life!" She knows it would be suicide to stay.

Finally she realizes what she must do. Summoning her strength, she raps him sharply on the back, catapulting him into space . . . and several feet closer to America. Regaining his footing, he lets out a yelp, more out of surprise than injury. Such a powerful punch for a woman of diminutive stature. An orphan has to be tough to survive so much loss and loneliness. Lately, however, it is becoming more and more difficult to maintain her stamina. A wave of nausea descends upon her, a painful reminder of her ill-timed pregnancy. She steadies herself.

He recovers his balance. "All right already. I'll go. But I don't like it. I don't like it one bit."

"Since when do you have to like it? Since when do you have to like anything? You just have to do it." She hurries past him as he paces the bareness of the kitchen floor.

"Leave everything behind . . . ," he mutters in disgust, although he knows that everything he is losing is in the future.

The only graduate of the village high school—that is how he is known to his jealous friends. It is a distinction, an honor that sets him apart from the laborers who are adept with their hands. But he has a keen mind and a fierce determination to use it to escape the degradation and the squalor. He tells himself that a Jew can rise above poverty and prejudice, even under the oppression of the czar—even in the midst of rampant anti-Semitism that spawns brutal, deadly pogroms. You just have to think your way out using your God-given wits.

"Nitwit!" she chides. "Stop your idle daydreaming and let's go."

He dutifully snatches the sack containing the few possessions that were spared liquidation to pay for passage to the New World.

Quickening his pace, he closes the gap, reaching her as she exits the portal. He shuts the door tightly, more out of habit than necessity. There is nothing left to protect. For a brief moment, his sweaty hand lingers on the door handle. Finally he reluctantly releases his grip and takes her hand. Together, they leave everything they ever knew— and would never know—behind them forever.

3

THE PRICE
of Poverty

June 7, 1959

Rap. Rap. Rap. My little knuckles knock on the peeling tenement door.

"Ma!" my mother calls loudly to her mother. "Can you hear me?"

A foreign voice echoes from within the apartment. "A minute. A minute," it shouts back hoarsely. My grandmother has been in America for almost fifty years now but can barely speak the language.

I grasp my mother's hand for courage. Such a strange place of rank smells and curious sights. The Lower East Side of New York bustles outside the tenement walls, indifferent to this six-year-old's struggle to maintain her composure and not appear too repulsed . . . or afraid.

"Now remember, be nice to your grandma," my mother prompts. "I'm sure she will be very happy to see you."

I stare down at the cracked tile floor. A tiny cockroach skirts around my patent leather shoe and vanishes under the apartment door. I smile to myself. He made it in first. He didn't have to stand here waiting forever in this stifling heat for a less-than-speedy human escort. I wonder if he is visiting his relatives inside. Are they any less scary than mine?

The door opens a crack, revealing a tiny, lined face trimmed in gold-rimmed glasses and stringy, gray hair. "A minute. A minute." She fiddles with the lock, her knobby, arthritic hands fumbling hopelessly with the chain. It seems like an eternity.

My mother finally speaks, her question stating the obvious. "Ma, are you having trouble?"

"A minute. A minute." A minute is becoming an hour.

Suddenly, mercifully, the chain is released and the door begins to swing open. My mother embraces the fragile woman who has fought her way to freedom. "Ma, I'm glad you're using that chain. You never know what dreck is out there, especially in this neighborhood." As if this flimsy lock could protect my grandmother from the perils of life.

"Bossala, Bossala!" my grandma exclaims as she wraps her withered arms around me before I can wriggle away. Her stained nightgown brushes my nose with the suffocating smell of mothballs. I can't decide what I dislike most—to hear my name in a foreign language or to be smothered in a hug by this alien relative.

"Let's not stand here by the door," my mother prompts. "Let's go into the kitchen and sit."

I reluctantly follow, being careful not to bump into the multitude of cardboard boxes and debris littering the long, narrow hall or to crush the cockroaches that are scurrying about unhampered. They seem particularly animated today. Maybe we've stepped into a welcoming party for the relative who slipped in ahead of us. It is intriguing how these little creatures take over every nook and cranny of this dilapidated apartment. They race over shelves and sink, tables and chairs as if they own the place, barely noticing the human intruders . . . and vice versa.

"Sit, Ma," my mother pleads.

"Oy, oy," my grandmother whines. It is an effort just moving that body through space. The same body that made it all the way from the shtetls of czarist Russia to the streets of America can hardly make it to the chair.

"Do you want to take a pill?" my mother asks in a worried tone.

"No, no." My grandma waves her hand in disgust. "No help. No help," she says, pointing to the dozens of medicine bottles on the table. It is hard to tell how much of her pain is due to debilitating illness . . . or to life in general.

"So, how's Stan?" my mother inquires, hoping to be told something positive for once about her recalcitrant brother.

"Ach," Grandma grunts, waving her hand again in disgust, beginning to mutter in Yiddish.

This is my cue. It is now time to make my long-awaited exit. They will be involved in conversation for hours, using strange sounds and dramatic gestures to communicate things that are not intended for my young ears. I make my getaway, barely hearing my mother say, "Beverly, maybe you can sit on the sofa and do your homework."

"Okay," I reply, knowing that I have much greater adventures to pursue. This strange, disordered place is an exotic wilderness, and I am on safari. Everything is fair game. I can search in drawers and cupboards, on shelves and tables, discovering oddly shaped buttons, thimbles, string, and even pennies. Whatever prized possessions I bag, I bring expectantly to my grandmother in hopes of gaining ownership. She always responds generously, "Take it. Take it," over the protests of my mother. With delight, I place the cherished objects in my pocket for further examination at home, where I don't have such pressing business. For now, the search must go on. Time is so limited.

Nothing off-limits here, except for one small room off to the side of the living room. It holds great mystery. From what I have gathered, it was my grandfather's bedroom before he died. What remains in there is anybody's guess. I was once able to sneak a peek when my grand-mother made one of her rare expeditions out of the kitchen to his room. Without human occupants to disturb the furnishings, it looked uncharacteristically neat and out of place. Even the cockroaches didn't dare enter it.

I have gleaned that, even in life, this was not a very approachable area of the apartment. I have been told that my grandfather was aloof, a dreamer, spending many nights in the teahouses discussing politics and literature after working all day as an unsuccessful pushcart fruit peddler. To his dying day, he maintained his integrity—and his poverty—by selling only the fruit that was in good condition. The bruised fruit he would give away to someone who seemed needier. While his intentions were noble, his idealism was out of place in a dog-eat-dog existence where the consequence of such honesty was starvation.

Nevertheless, honor seemed to be the only thing my grandfather felt he had left. And he guarded it scrupulously. This is not to say that others purposely set out to be dishonest. But in this self-contained Jewish ghetto, which was more densely populated than even the most crowded areas of Bombay, provisions were scarce and "ingenuity" was rewarded. The immigrants came to America bearing few possessions, having sold most of what they owned to purchase tickets for passage to the New World. They bore makeshift sacks on their backs to transport their few remaining valuables, such as feather pillows and candlesticks. Once in their new homeland, they used their sacks for peddling. From sack to pushcart to store. That was the progression from poverty to prosperity.

But not everyone made it that far, particularly the intellectuals who had fled the pogroms with lofty ideas but few down-to-earth skills. They combined to form the only intellectual working class ever created in America. These poet-peddlers struggled to make a living from second-class goods deemed unacceptable for uptown consumption. Stuffing their pushcarts to capacity with every conceivable type of merchandise, they barked and bartered, hustled and haggled until every last item was sold. They had no choice but to try to sell it all off each day. There was little room to store the items until the next morning.

Fruit peddlers, who handled perishable items, had an even more difficult plight due to bruising and spoilage. To recoup some of their inevitable losses, many would arrange their double-decker carts with such symmetry and style that unwary customers would willingly pay more. However, these inventive practices did not always protect such clever merchants from potential disaster. For these poor peddlers were destined to watch as some overweight yenta pushed and prodded, fingered and fumbled her way through the fruit cart like a proctologist on a rampage. All the merchant could do was shout less-than-poetic insults at her, such as schnorrer, in hopes of intimidating her into stopping the carnage. Invariably, she would not be satisfied until every single piece of fruit fell victim to her impeccable scrutiny. Then, having completed her selection, she would proceed to haggle, claiming indignantly that she was being overcharged for bruised fruit that, in reality, she herself had pummeled during the plum pogrom—not so inadvertently, of course. My grandfather was not cut out to be a crafty peddler dealing with such insufferable schnorrers. "Integrity over income" was the motto he preached to his starving family. Tragically, this promising idealistic intellectual failed miserably as a provider, having been done in by bruised bananas.

"Beverly, are you working on your homework?" my mother shouts from the kitchen.

"Yeah," I reply, pocketing the few new treasures I have amassed. It is time to retrieve my schoolbook before my mother discovers my delinquency. As one of three first graders chosen to participate in an advanced reading group, I cannot afford to slack off. My mother enthusiastically encourages my academic pursuits, maybe in part because she wasn't given such opportunities. I open my reader and begin to sound out the words. Yiddish phrases emanating from the kitchen punctuate my pronunciations.

My mind drifts as I envision my mother arriving at school at age five speaking only Russian and Yiddish. It must have been so embarrassing to be among English-speaking children who could not understand her, and vice versa. Spurred on by a deep desire to assimilate, she quickly learned to speak and read English.

Unfortunately, the language barrier was not her only obstacle. For she was deprived of even the basic necessities of life. One day, she was forced to wear her brother's shirt when no other attire was available. The principal sent her home that morning in shame. She never forgot that humiliating experience. Nor the time that she had to attend school with a shaved head after she suffered a terrible reaction to lice medication.

But perhaps her worst school years were spent having to wear a heavy steel back brace to correct scoliosis of the spine. She lived in constant dread of discovery, afraid that, through an inadvertent pat on the back, a particularly observant schoolmate would detect the screws and heavy metal bulging under her blouse and expose her secret. Her fear of being a social outcast was compounded by the stigma of having been stricken with rheumatic fever during her early school years. Because of the seriousness of her illness, she had not been allowed to attend school or play with her peers. Even when she was well enough to return to normal activity, she was unable to keep pace, having been deprived of learning such childhood activities as riding a bicycle, roller-skating, and playing team sports.

Mom enters the room with a flushed face. It is not unusual for my mother and grandmother to have heated discussions. And this is one of those days. The Yiddish Bowl is apparently at halftime now, and the participants have retreated to their respective mental locker rooms to plan their strategies.

"Beverly, are you hungry?"

I try to assess the state of my stomach.

"No, not really," I reply.

"Well, think of where you might like to eat when your father comes."

A sandpaper voice summons her back to the kitchen. She rejoins my grandmother. I gather from my mother's grin that she is winning the argument. I hope she takes the game. Victors are much more palatable dinner companions.

"Now, let's see, what do I feel like eating tonight?" I ask myself without much enthusiasm. It is amazing how nonchalant I am about dinner. Maybe it's because I have never had to miss a meal in my life. My mother has seen to that, maybe because she had to miss so many. I stand up and stretch, peering into the kitchen where the third quarter is under way. A few kitchen items are drying in the dish drainer. The remaining dishes, stacked on the shelf above the sink, are layered in dust. I wonder what it was like when those plates lined that dining room table, servicing a family of five. As I stand pondering, blurry images of phantom children emerge from behind the chairs. I blink, trying to clear my eyes to get a better view . . .

"Sophie, give me back my schoolbook!"

"I don't have it."

"Yes, you do."

" No, I don't."

"Sophie, give Stan his book," the woman in the white apron demands.

"But I don't have it!"

Stan locates his book under the newspaper on the chair. His father must have inadvertently covered it when he finished reading the Jewish Daily Forward *after dinner. No apologies made. None accepted.*

"Go to bed," their mother yells, waving them off like unwelcome guests. "Risa, help them get ready for bed."

A dark-haired girl with rosy cheeks emerges from behind the china closet where she has been carefully dusting the bric-a-brac. She is the firstborn and has the most demanding responsibilities. Lately, she is becoming even more burdened due to her mother's failing health. Her intrepid mother, who made it all the way to America while pregnant with her, is gradually succumbing to worsening symptoms of pain and fatigue. Regretfully, she must delegate more and more work to her oldest child.

All three siblings climb into bed and huddle together. It is the dead of winter and there is no heat except for the old stove, which cannot warm the long, frigid night. They will have to rely on body heat to keep them from freezing.

Hours have passed. Risa lies motionless, her eyes wide open as she stares at the cracked plaster on the wall. Her stomach is grumbling, still hungry after a meager dinner. Her limbs are stiff from remaining in the same position for hours. Yet she dare not move from the spot she has warmed on the pillow because the cloth surrounding her head has turned icy cold. Bedbugs scurry across the covers, unnoticed by the oblivious occupants. A cat suddenly races across the room, pouncing upon a large furry creature. It is a rodent, and the feline warrior has just captured another meal. The family rat catcher has earned her keep.

Risa feels an urgency to relieve herself but dares not venture to the bathroom. It is in the hall, shared by three other families, and she does not wish to face the cold and dark alone. Besides, there may not be sufficient newspaper or rags set aside at this hour for their customary use as an inexpensive alternative to toilet paper. She forces herself to think of other, more pleasant things.

Her mind drifts to last spring, when her mother surprised her with a porcelain doll. What a miracle to be given such a precious gift for which her mother had saved for so long. It was a most special doll, with a delicate face and lace dress. Risa smiles as she remembers her delight in holding the doll close to her. Suddenly, a crash pierces her reverie. Her shattered expression reveals her terror as she recalls the fragile treasure smashing against the hard wooden floor. How was she to know that the precious doll would slip so easily from her hands as she attempted to undress it to see what was underneath? A child's curiosity comes at a horrendous price. "Risa, look what you did!" her mother shouted in a punishing, unforgiving tone. "I will never buy you another doll."

"And she never did," I whisper to myself as the images begin to fade.

"Beverly, why are you standing there looking so sad?" My mother jars me back to reality. I stare at the gentle smile and loving eyes of the little girl who was never given another doll. Oh, how I wish I could buy my mother a doll right now! I run to embrace her, burying my face in her skirt while trying to hold back the flood of tears. I desperately hope she will not see me crying.

Suddenly, there's a knock at the door. "Risa?"

"Mac?"

It's my father. As my mother turns to open the door, I make my escape to the living room where I can tend to my emotions in private.

My father enters the kitchen in a rush with a tense look on his face. "Ready to go, Risa?" His words sound more like a demand than a question.

34

"In a minute, Mac," she reassures him.

My father looks noticeably uncomfortable and out of place in these surroundings. Having grown up in a slightly more fashionable part of New York City, the Bronx, he was able to escape the stigma of the infamous Lower East Side, where the inhabitants would be the first to admit that success meant "getting out." To my mother, my father represented an escape from deprivation and an opportunity for a better life. Not only was he somewhat better off economically, but his fun-loving, energetic personality was an antidote to the never-ending desperation and despair plaguing her struggling family. He brought life and a chance at happiness into her drab existence. This good-looking, red-headed staff sergeant was just the Prince Charming she needed to carry her away on a white horse—or rather an electric horse.

He, on the other hand, had been haunted by his lifelong nemesis—stuttering. As a young child, he would begin in earnest to form words, but they would come out in spurts and sputters like the backfiring of a car. Words became his enemy, betraying him at every attempt at expression. He dreaded the moments he had to spend in class. With sweat pouring down his forehead, he would watch the clock over the blackboard tick away the seconds. He'd pray that, this day, the bell would ring and he would escape just in the nick of time before he was called upon to speak.

Outside of class, he was subject to the constant ridicule and insults of not only his peers but also of his older brother. His parents did not intervene in the affairs of their five children. In fact, they provided little attention. As a boy, my father once made the mistake of placing his hand upon his father's arm. He was summarily slapped for seeking even this modicum of affection from his stern, distant parent.

Eventually, my father learned to protect himself, participating in fistfights between Jews and other minority gangs. He was strong and wiry. And his punches landed in perfect rhythm, unlike his broken words. He also learned to sing and accompany himself on the ukulele. Lyrics flowed effortlessly from his lips and won him the praise he so craved. To my mother, my father's words were music to her ears. And to him, she was the music for his words. For she articulated so beautifully and eloquently the phrases he was unable to say that she actually would make them sing.

In her warmth and acceptance, he found long-awaited validation. It didn't matter to him that she came from the ghetto of the Lower East Side. Nor to her that he was a stutterer. Neither saw the stigma in the other . . . only the strength. They had met at a dance where neither of them had planned to be that night. Yet they knew it was meant to be.

I peer into the kitchen. My mother has retrieved her coat and is reaching for her purse, a sign of imminent departure. I gather the treasures my grandmother gave me to keep and brush by her in a flash. I hope to elude Grandma's grasp and spare myself another mothball hug. My father rushes out the door while my mother lingers for a few departing Yiddish words. I reach for her hand as we make our way down the dilapidated stairs into the June sun, which is beginning to set.

"Mac, where did you park the car?" my mother yells to my father, who is already halfway down the block. Not stopping to answer, he points his finger forward. My mother and I quicken our pace in an attempt to catch up. Cars line the streets where pushcarts and horse-drawn carriages once stood. The raucous bedlam of the once teeming ghetto has diminished somewhat. Yet some reminders of old times remain. Many stores still display Hebrew and Yiddish signs. Rows of tenements still stand, having escaped the bulldozer, at least for the moment. But high-rises dot the landscape, a portent of things to come. Urban renewal will have its way.

My mother and I pass by the pickle barrels where we stopped earlier to buy half-sour five-cent pickles. This has always been one of our favorite treats. Whenever we partake of this delicacy, we reach into the huge wooden barrels filled with luscious pickled cucumbers and pick the fattest and most juicy ones. Then we devour the crunchy, moist treats with gusto, pickle juice dribbling down our chins. Our mouths salivate and sting from the sour delight for minutes thereafter as we savor the memory. But considering my father's pace, we dare not stop again today to indulge ourselves.

We walk on past the bagel store where we also shopped earlier. Looking in through the glass window, I can see our favorite little old lady fingering the delicious onion and sesame bialies and bagels. At her age, her nimble hands are still deftly kneading the dough into perfectly formed circles at record speed. My mouth waters as I remember the delectable onion bialy from this morning. Just the aroma emanating from the shop is enough to draw in a salivating person to beg for a bite. But we must continue onward.

Suddenly we spot the candy shop on the corner. My mother has been waiting for this all day. She yells to my father to stop. He turns around, expecting to see an ambulance or some other emergency vehicle that would justify a halt to his plans.

"Mac, I just want to go in here for a minute," she states with conviction.

My father eyes her, assessing just how adamant she is about this detour. When he sees her unflinching determination, he yields to her wishes. We all head for the door.

The candy store is a sort of family shrine, which always comes with my mother's legendary chocolate story. She relishes the recounting of this gruesome childhood tale as much for her catharsis as for our enlightenment. The story begins with an invitation from a neighborhood boy who frequently asked her to accompany him to the candy store to buy a piece of chocolate. My mother, who had no money and could not partake of such a delicacy, would always tag along, hoping to be given a bite. She would accompany this "fat kid"—that was his name, apparently—all the way to the candy shop, savoring the thought of delicious chocolate melting in her mouth. When they finally arrived, he would pull a shiny coin from his pocket and exchange the precious possession for a luscious piece of dark semisweet chocolate—her favorite. Then, as she kept her hopes raised to the very end, he would proceed to eat every last morsel right in front of her. She never received one bite.

Her memories of such torture fuel her determination that her family never know such feelings of deprivation. So we have arrived at the candy shop to load up on discount chocolate, nuts, and dried apricot rolls. We weave through the aisles past sacks of nuts bordered by open boxes of chocolate in every variety: chocolate-covered orange and cherry jellies, square chocolates layered with marshmallows, chocolate-covered raisins and peanuts. The selection is endless. We leave with lots and lots of goodies bulging from a huge shopping bag. It is a month's supply that will be consumed within a week. But my mother's satisfaction will linger far longer.

We finally reach our 1955 blue Chevy sedan, and I climb into the familiar vinyl seat, happy to be going home at last. Surrounded by the aroma of fresh chocolate, I am immersed in memories of the day. As I tug at my pockets that hold the bounty I have amassed from the scavenger hunt at Grandma's apartment, I think of the toys and pets I have waiting for me at home . . . and of the shattered face of the broken porcelain doll.

No matter how much I try to imagine what my mother's life was like when she was my age, I cannot fathom the extent of her suffering. She has spared me any real inkling of such hardship and deprivation by trying to provide me with what she could not have. I wonder why I am given so much and she was given so little. Didn't she say her prayers to God every night as I do? She must have, given her strict religious upbringing. Maybe God didn't hear her. Is our house closer to heaven than is the Lower East Side? Maybe she should have shouted. Was she too weak from hunger to raise her voice? Can God detect whispers . . . or maybe even silent hopes? Does he really listen? Does he really care? If he does care, why doesn't he answer? If he doesn't care, why do we pray?

The familiar, tree-lined streets of suburbia welcome us home. The colorful shingled houses beckon us back to a world of neatly mowed lawns, plastic swimming pools, and sandboxes.

As I snuggle with my teddy bear in my cozy bed, I thank the Lord for my family and for bringing me home again. A tear trickles down my face onto the warm pillow as I ask God to please keep me safe . . . so Mama won't ever have to see me break.

4

A REFUGE
of Love

Eve of Yom Kippur, 1963

"Beverly, hurry up and set the table. The sun will be setting soon."

I drop my sixth-grade math book on the desk and run to the kitchen.

"Sorry, Mom." I struggle to recover from the grueling mental gymnastics of endless arithmetic brainteasers in order to refocus on a more meaningful pursuit—dinner.

It will be an especially luscious dining bonanza—the traditional meal before Yom Kippur. On this sacred holiday, the Jewish Day of Atonement, we are required to observe a day-long fast. The object of the pre–Yom Kippur culinary experience is to feast in preparation for the famine. We become camels, loading up on precious supplies before heading out to the arid and foreboding desert. The thought of being just one bagel short of making it is too painful to bear. So we eat two just to be sure.

"Should I set the table with the good dishes?" I ask eagerly.

"Yes, and we'll eat in the dining room."

Great. We get a chance to actually sit in that hallowed room, which is usually reserved for more civilized, worthy people. They are commonly called "company." On this special evening, I will gratefully escape the labors of sitting on that sticky vinyl chair that I can never quite steady on the linoleum kitchen floor.

I carefully open the glass-paned door of the beautifully carved apricot-colored breakfront. This cherished piece of furniture has become my mother's "ark of the coveted," for it houses all her prized possessions, mostly amassed since her marriage with the little disposable income she could scrape together. She collects such finery for its intrinsic beauty, not its material worth. It is a tradition passed down from her mother, who, even in the midst of dire poverty, managed to scrape together enough money to fill a small china closet with a few pieces of inexpensive porcelain bric-a-brac. It was a great source of pride and beauty in a household drowning in the degradation of tenement life.

For years I have watched my mother faithfully and lovingly caress each piece of china and cut glass with a special cloth. With each new acquisition seems to come renewed reassurance that she is one step further from the deprivation of the ghetto. I gingerly reach in and start unloading the precious dinnerware.

"If I didn't get home so late," my mother continues, "I would not have had to rush so much."

I do not respond. She is not really addressing me but her archenemy—the family business. She is once again chiding our clothing store as if it were a naughty member of the family, an errant child who has spoiled her holiday dinner out of spite. It is not bad enough that the family loses needed income every time the store must close early for a holiday. Or that it must remain open on Saturday, the Jewish

Sabbath, because it is the busiest retail day of the week. But the family livelihood, which takes on a life of its own, *constantly* intrudes upon her religious and secular life.

"If it weren't for those few stragglers that came in at the last minute, we would have gotten home at least an hour ago."

Wishful thinking, Mom, I muse but maintain my silence. I have learned not to intervene in the battles between my mother and the store. This source of sustenance that puts food on our table remains a hornet's nest of agonizing ambivalence. It has become a bitter rival that is to blame for the strains in her marriage, which has to double as a business partnership, the scant social life she can barely have, and the half-finished housework she cannot afford to pay someone else to do. Worst of all, it deprives her of precious time she wishes she could spend with my brother and me.

"Do you want to help me bring the food into the dining room?" Her voice softens as she directs herself to a human presence.

"Sure, Mom." The aroma of the delicious delicacies is enough to bring me running back to the kitchen, where the scrumptious Jewish delights are sprawled over every possible inch of counter space.

"I hope I made enough," she says, apologetically. Enough? My mother could feed the troops at Valley Forge and still have enough leftovers for the British.

"It's fine," I reassure her.

The clattering of platters on the finely polished dining room table is enough to summon one of the troops—a boy scout from Pack 116 whose purple ceramic fish hangs proudly next to the potato masher.

"Eddie, where's your father?"

"Dad, dinner!" my brother screams at the top of his lungs.

Thanks a lot, Eddie. Mom didn't need you to scream clear across the house. She could have done that herself! Why are brothers always so loud and annoying? I know boys are supposed to mature more slowly than girls. But he is almost four years older than I am. Why doesn't he hurry up already? Besides, it is Yom Kippur. Can't we be a nice, well-mannered, quiet family like everyone else's for just one night?

"Risa, now?" My dad's voice echoes through the hall as he rushes to the dining room.

"Yes, Mac, now. Please sit down, and I'll serve."

My father surveys the table, seriously assessing the situation for imminent dining activity. He finally decides to be seated. It is always a tough call for him, knowing when to actually stop what he is doing and sit down for dinner. He is chronically overwhelmed by the responsibilities of the family business, which does not provide enough income to hire much additional help. Even while at home he spends almost every waking hour serving this all-consuming master. Besides, patience is not one of his virtues, and waiting is nothing short of torture. His reputation for punctuality has earned him the nickname Railroad Mac.

My mother, on the other hand, tends to have a somewhat more flexible approach to time. Knowing this all too well, my father greets her pronouncements of "time for dinner" with the utmost of suspicion. Is it really time *now* for dinner, one minute from *now,* or ten minutes from *now?* His obvious skepticism always annoys my mother, who snaps back such quips as, "I told you that I am serving *now,* and I am serving *now.*"

I have watched this battle for years and have decided that the problem lies in the interpretation of the word *now.* My mother uses the word in so many contexts: *now,* as in immediately; *now,* as in after I do just a few more things; and *now*, as in I intend it to be this minute even though it probably will be a lot longer than that but I'll still use the word *now* to show my good intentions. Railroad Mac, who expects everyone to meet all obligations on a railroad schedule, finds Mom's creative definitions to be absolutely intolerable.

Minutes have passed with no sign of my mother. Finally, we hear the dreaded phrase, "Wait a minute!" emanating from the kitchen. Across the great divide, my mother shouts, "I need to light the candles before it's too late!" Oh no. The word *now* has to be redefined again.

Dad looks up in disgust but dares not move from the table. He is not about to take on God as his next opponent. Traditionally the candles are lit after the meal, before the official start of Yom Kippur at sunset. This is a rule that my mother scrupulously obeys, despite business obligations that invariably threaten to derail her plans to leave the store early during the High Holy Days. But this year, the store has finally won out. It is now almost sunset, and she faces a terrible dilemma. If she waits until after dinner to light the candles, the sacred ceremony would take place way past sunset. Violating such an important Yom Kippur tradition would be too much for her to bear. She is already distressed that we will be unable to finish our meal before sundown. So she has apparently decided to light the candles first. Yet I can see from her tortured expression that she is left with agonizing ambivalence.

"Beverly, will you bring the candlesticks to the table?"

I jump out of my seat, happy to escape the tension of sitting next to my still unfed father. I retrieve the cherished objects from their place of honor on the shelf. My mother hurries out of the kitchen with a box of candles in her hand and disappears into the bedroom. I can hear her opening the bottom drawer of her dresser, searching for a head covering. My father is nervously and hungrily tapping his fingers on the table, just millimeters from the precious chicken, which he dares not touch. I can tell that he is engaged in complicated calculations of just how many minutes he has already lost sitting there and what he could have accomplished if he had just guessed the right meaning of the word *now* this time.

"Will someone please turn off the lights?" my mother requests as she rushes into the dining room.

My brother has been unusually quiet for the past few minutes, probably fearful of further irritating my father with needless conversation. However, the unruly bundle of energy that is my brother can control itself for just so long. Just as I reach for the light switch, Mount Eddie starts to erupt. Perfect timing, as usual. My mother's annoyed expression cuts him off at the pass. She usually lets him get away with such annoying chatter. Thankfully, even he must be subdued on Yom Kippur.

As I dim the lights, we are quickly immersed in darkness and silence. How I wish I could flick a switch anytime I want and bring down the curtain on all the noise and tension in this struggling, barely middle-class, suburban family. Overwhelmed, overextended, overstimulated, we are constantly running from past demons and imagined foes who threaten to overtake us if we are not ever vigilant to work our way up—and out of their path.

As she lights the candles, my mother is clothed in a gown of light. She circles her hands over the dancing flames and gently places her fingers over her eyes. Silently she begins to pray. The dining room, which just seconds before had been filled with sound and fury, has been transformed into a holy sanctuary. Bathed in an iridescent glow, she transcends earth to heaven. We are privileged intruders, witnessing a sacred private interlude, the depth of which we can barely imagine. This is not just an awesome display of one fragile human soul's proclamation of love for her God. It is a mystical and gut-wrenching moment, when a mere mortal dares to enter the presence of an omnipotent deity to beseech him to bless the seemingly insignificant beings surrounding this Yom Kippur table and to watch over the dearly departed, who, being mere dust, have passed on to a place unknown. I have always believed that this intrepid and passionately devoted mother bravely protests as she lays the long family history of enormous suffering at the feet of the Lord—and even dares to ask why.

A tear trickles between her fingers and splashes onto the linen tablecloth. We watch, motionless, as her shoulders begin to shudder and the sobbing grows louder. I sense that she has reached the prayers for her mother, who died only last year from a torturous, lingering bout with stomach cancer. I imagine that she is bringing to the Lord that well of unspeakable sorrow, which only in rare moments breaks through the dam of silence under the enormous weight of intense mourning. I am certain that she is grieving more for the horrible life Grandma had to endure than for her death.

My mother's trembling, wet hands drop from her face and reach for the covering still balanced precariously upon her head. No one moves. We look into the eyes that stare past us. They convey a knowing vulnerability and pain we will never understand. Suddenly her glance falls upon me. Her face softens into a faint, loving smile as she attempts to shield me from the saddest expression I have ever seen. Deeply sighing with resignation, in a tear-stained voice, she murmurs, "Let's eat."

My brother is the first one to jump up to turn on the lights. He follows Mom into the kitchen, chattering about something irrelevant. "From sanctuary to circus," I mutter. Why couldn't I have had a sister?

We proceed to the kitchen to continue carting the endless culinary delights to the dining room. The sight of this parade of scrumptious entrées fires the starting pistol, triggering the stomach juices to flow. I stare at the food with lust. This is it. Let the games begin!

The marathon of a Yom Kippur fast must be approached with careful strategy, developed over years of experience. Painful memories of the Yom Kippur day Heartbreak Hill remain forever in one's gut. There is always a belief that this year's new and improved dining regime will fend off those dreaded hunger pains. It never works. Inevitably, at 3 P.M. the next day, the stomach roars and registers its greatest protest as the pitifully weakened and deprived organ groans and grinds its way over Heartbreak Hill. Remarkably, once over the hump, hunger seems to diminish as sunset approaches. It is as if the challenge has been won and the victorious organ has proved its independence from baser earthly instincts.

I survey the feast, calculating the quantities I plan to devour and the order of consumption. I fill my plate and my mouth.

"Another drumstick, Beverly?" my mother inquires as the endless chicken parts are circulated around the table.

I consider this question in light of my plan. Do I dare refuse? What if I am one chicken leg short of making it to the finish line? "Sure, Mom. Thanks."

By now, my stomach is filled beyond capacity, and I am sick of food. But I have to stick to the plan. I must tolerate feeling overstuffed tonight to avoid hunger pangs tomorrow. I reach for the challah, the traditional Jewish bread that always ends my feast. Its bulky texture reassures me that if I haven't devoured the requisite number of chicken parts, these last morsels will surely suffice.

Finally it is over. Chicken bones and various unrecognizable substances are draped over the plates like party streamers. It is time for the enormous job of cleanup. I can hardly budge under the weight of my bulging stomach. I pry myself out of the chair and grab the platter containing the half-eaten chicken carcass. I can barely stand the sight, particularly since I have just wolfed down numerous parts of its unfortunate relatives. I head for the kitchen where dishwashing is already under way. We all pitch in until every last utensil is put away and the kitchen no longer contains any hint of its customary use. For the remainder of the holiday, it will be just another place for reading and conversation.

Observing Yom Kippur in our household not only means that we must fast but also that we must adhere to many other rules that my mother has set in place based on her understanding of Conservative Jewish practices. Conservative Jews attempt to strike a happy medium between the strict Orthodox and liberal Reform branches of Judaism. Abandoning her Orthodox upbringing to escape the rigidity of the old ways and adopt a more secular way of life, my mother has had to struggle with just how much she can comfortably depart from tradition and still feel like a practicing Jew. It is a balancing act that leaves her in a constant state of uncertainty and guilt.

Orthodox Jews do not work on Yom Kippur. This literally means no work of any kind, including such nontaxing tasks as turning on an electrical appliance, starting a car engine, or even turning on the lights. My mother has instituted a similar rule . . . with certain key exceptions.

For example, we are allowed to turn on the lights. This she considers to be a practical and necessary concession. But television and radio are strictly off-limits. I can never quite understand this, for, in my world, watching television is just as much a necessity as turning on the lights. But no negotiation works. It is a total blackout. In fact, my mother is so adamant on this point that she has created a strange Yom Kippur tradition—the annual after-dinner walk.

We embark upon our evening stroll, ostensibly designed to walk off the heavy meal. However, the real mission is to patrol this Jewish neighborhood in search of Yom Kippur violators. From our vantage point on the sidewalk, we peer into the living-room windows of one Jewish neighbor after another to ferret out those brazen transgressors who actually have the chutzpah to watch television on Yom Kippur. These religious felons are unceremoniously labeled goyim and cataloged in my mother's mind for future reference.

We return home to face the seemingly endless hours together. Yet despite the trials and sacrifice, I actually love the holiday of Yom Kippur. For, stripped of life's clutter, trappings, and intrusions, we are free to relate in unfettered ways. Despite it all, we have made it through the madness and mayhem of another year of life and can take comfort and refuge in the company of our loved ones once again. Even my brother becomes somewhat more tolerable . . . a Yom Kippur miracle.

Ultimately, there is an abiding realization that we are all in this together—no matter what . . .

5

HOLIDAY
Heroics

Yom Kippur morning, 1963

The shrill of an insistent alarm clock pierces my consciousness, stirring me from a deep sleep. I reach for the alarm button to silence the intrusion but find it already disengaged. *That's strange. Wait a minute. I didn't set the alarm last night, not on Yom Kippur.* The noise stops abruptly. I have a sudden revelation. Across the hall, my father has silenced the electronic rooster on *his* night table.

Dad is our resident goy, a barely observant Jew who tolerates Mom's rituals more out of respect for her than for God. In my father's world, she is the higher authority. During occasions such as this, when someone has to break the rules and set the alarm on Yom Kippur, Dad is pressed into service. This morning he summons the flock.

Flock, rooster, chicken. A faint wave of nausea comes over me at the thought of poultry. Last night's chickenfest has taken its toll. My stomach gurgles, a faint complaint of past transgressions and an anticipation of the day's fast. No matter how many morsels I have managed to stuff into my body the evening before, I always feel hungry for breakfast. But the only substance that will reach this mouth today will be toothpaste, which will become surprisingly appetizing in the absence of culinary competitors. There will be no drink of water afterward. Toothbrushing must be followed only by a cursory rinse—no swallowing, just spitting. These are our Yom Kippur dental hygiene rules.

My dress for temple is hanging in the back of my closet, untouched since the last Jewish holiday. It is the frock of choice when nice and conservative is in order. It distresses me that I have nothing new to wear this year. Given the limited family finances, my mother cannot afford to buy me a dress every year for Rosh Hashanah and Yom Kippur—although purchasing a new outfit for these occasions seems to be the custom for many at our temple, where High Holy Day services tend to resemble an Yves Saint Laurent event.

On Yom Kippur we atone for our sins. Otherwise, we may not be inscribed in the Book of Life for the coming year. But if the truth be known, a far worse fate for many of these congregants would be to commit a fashion felony and make the "worst-dressed list." Women routinely parade around the grounds outside the sanctuary for as long as possible to attract would-be wardrobe admirers. When all sources of rave reviews have been exhausted, they take the show inside. There, amid the prayers, the displays continue through gestures and admiring glances. This unabashed exhibition of materialism on hallowed temple grounds always makes me cringe. Yet as I stare at my well-worn dress, I still can't help worrying what my friends will think of my familiar frock.

My mother rushes into the room, affixing a pearl earring to her lobe. "Beverly, you look very nice."

"Thanks, Mom. Do you think anyone will remember that I wore

this same dress last year on the High Holy Days?" I ask, trying to hide my conflicting emotions.

"It looks very pretty on you, Beverly. I doubt anyone will remember."

My mother never places much emphasis on material things. Unlike so many of her cohorts who grew up in dire poverty and later joined the ranks of the nouveau riche, or at least the middle class, my mother resists the temptation to indulge in materialism to compensate for past deprivation. Instead she clings steadfastly to riches that surpass tangible wealth, such as moral character, compassion, and charity. She shares her bounty by embracing every living thing with such enthusiasm and warmth that anyone she touches cannot help being moved by the depth of her love and the extent of her kindness. Walking the earth as a philosopher-mother, she never misses the opportunity to shower willing listeners with Yiddish sayings that contain the wisdom of the ages, bequeathed to her from her mother. These are the treasures she values and has taught me to cherish, as well.

Emerging from my bedroom, I glance in the direction of my brother's room. "Hi, Eddie," I call.

No response. He is searching frantically for a small, blue-velvet pouch emblazoned with a gold Star of David. It contains a special yarmulke (head covering) and tallith (prayer shawl), given to him at his bar mitzvah. I remember all the glitter and commotion of that day when, at age thirteen, he was officially declared a man, according to the Jewish religion. I could never understand what all the fuss was about. According to me, he behaved like a two-year-old before the ceremony and didn't get much older afterward. I guess if they actually waited for him to grow up, the bar mitzvah boy would be an eighty-five-year-old grandfather already and my parents would be long gone. Then, who would be there to pay for the smorgasbord and to kvell (burst with pride) as he squeaked out the Haftarah (Scripture reading) from the pulpit? So the very wise rabbis, who are reputed to have the Wisdom of Solomon, probably picked an arbitrary age like thirteen just to get on with it.

"Mom!" Eddie yells to her across the house, making sure to wake up any neighbors who are attempting to sleep late on Yom Kippur, "I can't find my yarmulke!"

"Did you look in the bottom drawer of the credenza?" she shouts back, hoping not to have to interrupt her preparations for temple.

"Yeah. It's not there."

Mom persists. "It has to be there. Where else could it be?"

My mother has a point. This routine has become a classic from my "Greatest Hits of a Very Annoying Brother" album. Mom abandons what she is doing and rushes to his side. She reaches under the shirts, magically producing the prized possession. Another Yom Kippur miracle! Eddie looks sheepishly at her as if he has no clue that the pouch has been retrieved from the same spot in the same manner for the last several years. My mother smiles, trying to hide her annoyance. Sometimes, I think she has the patience of a saint . . . or perhaps more. After all, Father Damien only had to work with lepers, not brothers. I wonder if my brother's inability to find the pouch is because he is blinded by fear. What if he really did lose his bar mitzvah yarmulke and tallith? Would the Lord ever forgive him?

I never have to worry about such things. As a female, I am not required to wear these articles, which somehow symbolize exclusive male membership in the "club" of Judaism. I feel like a tagalong, tolerated—but not embraced—by my religion. My mother has told me that, in Orthodox synagogues, females are actually placed behind a curtain to separate them from males. I cannot understand the meaning of such a practice. Is it to protect the men from contamination? Of course, in the case of my brother, I would welcome a curtain . . . or the Berlin Wall, for that matter. Nevertheless, I wonder why Orthodox women are segregated and systemically excluded from important aspects of Judaism. Even more unsettling is that, from what my mother has told me, an Orthodox male must recite a daily morning prayer in gratitude that God did not make him a "heathen," a "brutish man," or a "woman"!

With no breakfast to delay our departure, we all head out the door for the long walk to temple. Yes, walk. Riding to temple is considered work because one has to turn on the motor, I think. I wonder why we can't press my father, our resident goy, into service once again. He could start the engine, and then we would all jump in, saving a walk of several miles to the temple. I would even turn my back as he turned the key, just to make sure I wouldn't be party to a Yom Kippur rule violation. But there is no room for argument. My mother chooses to follow the rule . . . and the rule is to walk. By the time we arrive at the temple, my toes are pinched and my feet are aching from all the work I did *not* do by walking.

We are always relieved to arrive at the temple. For, despite our weakness from the fast, we have made it through the long walk. But the true test of bravery is yet to come. For we arrive bearing no tickets for admission to the service. Unlike our Christian counterparts, Jews must purchase seats in advance to be allowed into the sanctuary. But my parents have a limited income and cannot afford the hefty price of continued temple membership, building-fund assessments, and High

Holy Day seats. Yet my mother must find a way for her family to worship. So, despite her embarrassment, she leads us to the temple each year on the High Holy Days, hoping she will be able to smuggle us into the service.

Mom has become expert at her craft. As we enter the temple lobby leading to the sanctuary, she eyes the forbidden doors, like a hawk stalking its prey. Slowly, we make our way to the entrance. It appears to be momentarily unguarded. What luck! Suddenly I feel a push at my back as I am whisked into the sanctuary just behind my brother.

Although masses of people surround us, there are still plenty of empty seats. The service began early this morning and, by now, tired or bored congregants have made their way to the hall, the bathroom, or home. There is still sufficient time to pray, however. Services take place throughout the day until the end of Yom Kippur at sunset. I eye my mother, who is expertly sizing up the situation. She seems to have a sixth sense that helps her to predict which seats are temporarily vacant versus those that can be relied upon to remain unclaimed. It is a test of skill she seems to relish.

She readies herself to stake her claim. "There!" she whispers, pointing to four vacant chairs in the next to last row on the right. We quickly seize the seats, trying to look as if we own them. Mom sighs with great relief, hoping that we will remain in these spots undisturbed. I glance at her with admiration. Despite all obstacles, she has managed to situate her family in the Lord's house on this most holy day of the year— even if she had to steal religion to do it!

For the first time since we arrived, I have an opportunity to relax and survey the situation. All is bedecked in white to signify purity. The rabbi and the cantor, who are adorned in special Yom Kippur attire, appear particularly holy in white. Even the Torah scrolls and the reader's table are covered in Yom Kippur white. Some of the congregants have chosen to follow suit in honor of this holy day. I imagine that God is really impressed by this gesture since, in this crowd, it is particularly courageous to wear white after Labor Day. The cantor is chanting plaintive Hebrew refrains as we reach for the prayer books.

The next challenge is to try to locate the correct page. This is no easy task. There are no programs to keep track of the sequence of events. There should be programs. After all, you need tickets! Mom looks around at the open prayer books in the laps of the adjacent congregants in an attempt to ascertain a page number. This does not go well. People are looking up at her with puzzled expressions. No one is on the same page. This is no surprise. Services on the High Holy Days can be quite chaotic and confusing. The activities on the pulpit seem to serve as a backdrop for people loitering in the aisles, coming and going to the bathroom, and making stops along the way to whisper loudly to each other.

The service will go on, with or without them. And, when all is said and done, they will return home feeling righteous and holy, having attended services on Yom Kippur. I stare at them with annoyance. We may have had to steal religion today . . . but their hypocrisy is a crime.

My mother starts to sing, having succeeded in finding the proper place in the prayer book. She catches my eye and points her finger to the page number. I quickly turn to that section with eager anticipation but find the page entirely covered with Hebrew letters. My spirits fall. I am reminded that I can't read Hebrew. I chose clarinet lessons instead.

I am saved, however, by the familiar chanting of the Al Chet breaking out all around me. This is such an important Yom Kippur prayer that we recite it in English so that everyone can be included. I join in for the recitation. The prayer recounts every imaginable transgression. The list is exhaustive. It is highly unlikely that any one of us has committed every single one of these sins. But we pray in the plural because all of these sins have been and are being committed, and we are all responsible for each other. I feel a particularly heavy burden as I look over at my brother, who is fidgeting with his yarmulke. According to Judaism, I am even responsible for him.

The service continues in Hebrew, and I rejoin the linguistically challenged who sit silently, trying not to look too bored or too stupid. I thumb through the prayer book, looking for something recognizable. Ah, I know this one . . . Avinu Malkenu, one of my favorite Yom Kippur prayers. Each of the many lines begins "Avinu Malkenu" ("Our Father, our King"), which makes it easy to learn and remember. I read some of the lines to myself in translation.

As I continue my expedition through the prayer book, I hear the voice of the rabbi announcing that he is about to deliver his sermon. He admonishes, "Anyone wishing to leave should leave now." The rabbi always delivers this presermon warning. I have thought it should be accompanied by a loud siren cautioning us all to duck and take cover. Actually, the reason for this stern rabbinical notification is that, once he begins the sermon, no one is allowed to speak, wander the aisles, or leave. Such activity is considered disrespectful and breaks the rabbi's concentration. He takes these transgressions very personally. Of course, this puts a crimp in the style of many talkative and meandering worshipers who can hardly tolerate such restrictions. Thus, they generally hightail it out of the sanctuary at the mention of the word *sermon*.

This morning the rabbi's announcement brings an unusually massive number of worshipers to their feet. You'd think the ark holding the sacred Torahs had just been opened, causing the mandatory rising of the whole congregation out of respect. The worshipers stream down the aisles, enthusiastically escaping the dreaded event. The rest of us remain in our seats, wondering if we will regret our decision to stay.

I brace myself for the long sermon ahead, trying to reassure myself that, although it may not be readily understandable, at least it is in English. This pleases us disenfranchised monolinguists in the crowd. The rabbi has developed repetitive dramatic phrases in hopes of maintaining our attention. One of his favorites is "the Jewish people," which he enunciates with great reverence and deliberateness. I suspect that this impressive delivery is not only to convey a special respect for us, but also to punctuate the ponderous paragraphs. As he reaches the climax, I make a mental note to discuss a few points with my mother during our walk home; although, I never remember such lofty intentions. Usually my starved brain cannot retain more than the all-consuming thought, *I am so hungry. I wish I could eat already.*

As we leave the temple, I know that food is exactly what my father has in mind. For him, the Yom Kippur fast is almost over. With ulcers comes the welcomed privilege of breaking the fast at lunchtime. My mother is convinced that my father's ulcers are a by-product of his impatient personality. So it must be particularly difficult for her to watch him break the Yom Kippur fast early because of a condition he could have avoided if he had just adopted a more flexible interpretation of the word *now.*

Breaking the fast early is not the only concession my father is allowed. Dad also partakes of milk with meat to soothe his acid-filled stomach. Mixing dairy with meat at our kosher table is a clear violation of Jewish dietary laws and a source of great discomfort for my mother. Not that she keeps a completely kosher kitchen. Unlike her Orthodox mother, Mom prefers not to keep the requisite two sets of dishes—one for dairy and one for meat. In her overburdened life, it is too impractical. But she primarily buys kosher food and refrains from purchasing pork. Yet she is lenient regarding other prohibited foods, such as shellfish. Conservative compromise can be quite confusing.

Such inconsistency frequently prompts me to question the whole system, much to her dismay. "Why can't we have milk with meat?" I ask. "It's not a kosher practice," she always replies. "But, why?" I persist. "It's the way we do things," she counters. "But I don't see why. It makes no sense," I insist. She inevitably becomes more and more annoyed. "It is tradition," she parries back, hoping this will be the final blow. But I always save my best punch for last. "We don't have two sets of dishes, only one. We occasionally eat shellfish, which isn't kosher, but we don't eat pork. What's the point of all these archaic rules anyway? The whole thing is hypocritical." This is enough to send my mother into a mild rage. She usually ends the argument with a low but extremely effective blow: "When you are under my roof, you will do things my way. Afterward you are on your own. If you want to turn into a goy like your father, be my guest." At age eleven, I can hardly pack my bags and head out the door to set up my own goyish home. So I usually retreat.

Actually, I cannot really fault my mother. She is trying desperately to hold on to her traditions and faith in the midst of a changing world. This is not the Lower East Side of my mother's childhood, which was more European than American. We live in an assimilated generation that is witnessing the old ways rapidly fading into the new. To her credit, my mother strives to adapt, while diligently retaining her Jewish identity in the process. In some ways, she welcomes the opportunity to adopt a more liberal perspective that requires less stringent adherence to Orthodox rituals. She still carries resentment that her mother would discard all leavened bread products on Passover rather than store them in cupboards for use at the holiday's end. When there was no money to replenish the supply, the family would go hungry. My mother is determined not to inflict upon her own family the severe, sometimes cruel religious restrictions she endured as a child.

As we arrive home, I head for my bedroom to change into something more comfortable. I hear the clattering of plates and silverware emanating from the kitchen as my father breaks his fast, much to his delight . . . and to the delight of his ulcers. Hearing these familiar culinary sounds, I begin to salivate like Pavlov's dog. I dare not go near the kitchen. Adding sight to sound will push me over the edge. Nevertheless, I begin to picture the forbidden food as it is placed upon his plate—the flaky tuna fish, the creamy mayonnaise, the fluffy challah. *Oh no, I must practice restraint!*

I pick up the book I have set aside for this Yom Kippur day. It is *Exodus* by Leon Uris, a long, action-filled adventure recounting the founding of the state of Israel. Such a compelling story is a perfect choice to combat hunger pains during the long afternoon. Yet I can't help returning to thoughts of my father sitting in the kitchen enjoying his lunch. I smile at the thought of Dad reaping the benefits of his impatience . . . while I try to find patience of my own.

"Beverly, will you be joining me for the Neilah service?" my mother asks as she approaches my bed.

I look up, unaware that it is late afternoon. I have spent the last three hours with the brave freedom fighters in the Warsaw ghetto and the stoic pioneers on kibbutzim in Israel. I hardly noticed my grumbling stomach as it made its way over Heartbreak Hill. At this late hour the hunger pains have begun to subside, attributable, most likely, to the victory that is close at hand. "Sure, Mom. I'd love to accompany you back to temple," I reply, trying to summon all the enthusiasm I can muster.

"Well, you'd better get ready. We don't have much time before we have to leave."

I get up from my bed, slightly lightheaded and weak. I hope I will catch my second wind so that I can survive the long walk back to temple for the closing Yom Kippur service.

Actually, I am pleased to take part in the prayers that end Yom Kippur, especially since I missed last night's Kol Nidre service, which began the holiday. At the start of Yom Kippur, we ask God for forgiveness for not keeping our vows to him. During the Yom Kippur service, we repent of our sins against God. For sins against others, we are required to approach our victims to ask for forgiveness. Only then can we say we have truly atoned for our transgressions.

The Neilah service at the end of Yom Kippur is our last chance to repent. It is the culmination of the Ten Days of Repentance, which begin on Rosh Hashanah, the Jewish New Year. During this time, God decides whether to inscribe us in the Book of Life. At the close of the Neilah service, the Book is sealed.

I arise and quickly ready myself to leave. My father and brother elect to stay home. They are eyeing the clock, hoping that the sun will set more quickly than usual tonight. My mother and I embark upon our walk back to temple, sharing our impressions of the day as we enjoy the warmth of the late-afternoon sun.

When we arrive at the temple, we find a much smaller crowd than was in attendance this morning. Earlier worshipers have long since departed, having paid their respects and cleansed their consciences for another year. We make our way toward the front of the sanctuary and locate a place to sit. But before we can settle in our seats, we are called to rise. We begin the long final stand in front of the open ark.

The Neilah service is distinctive in that the ark remains open from beginning to end to signify that the gates of heaven are open at this time. The mood is solemn. Unlike in the earlier, crowded service, where there was more commotion than prayer, congregants are now pensive and unified as they come before the Lord one last time in confession and deep repentance. There is a sense of urgency as we plead for forgiveness. Standing in front of the open ark containing the sacred scrolls, praying these heart-wrenching prayers, a feeling of awe and devotion fills my soul. My mother reaches for my hand and holds it tightly. The cantor raises the shofar, the ram's horn, indicating that Yom Kippur is officially over.

With tears running down my face, I smile at my mother. She, who has experienced so many Yom Kippur holidays, beams back with a relieved and thankful expression. I feel privileged to share this ethereal moment with her. Standing there in the rays of the setting sun filtering into the sanctuary, we are in a heavenly interlude. Purified by repentance, fortified by our victory over baser instincts, and filled with compassion for those less fortunate who hunger out of circumstance, not choice, we leave the temple with new resolve to make a conscious effort to live a more righteous, holy, and grateful life in the year to come.

As we set out for home under a clear, evening sky, we are bathed in the warm glow of twilight. By the time we near our destination, the sky has turned a deep velvet blue. We quicken our pace as the lights shining in the kitchen beckon us home. Our precious retreat must end, for our everyday responsibilities await us.

We have devoted this day to reconciliation with our Lord, our family, and others. Having repented of our sins and faced our human vulnerabilities, we have found renewed strength and deeper faith in God. We pray that we have been inscribed in the Book of Life. Yet we know not what the coming year will bring. I can't help wondering if God has taken note of our sacrifice, repentance, and prayers. Does such a seemingly distant, almighty, and incomprehensible God really take a personal interest in our lives?

As we stand before our front door, I glance at my mother's serene face, grateful to have gained a glimpse of what it means to her to be a Jew. In the light of the moon, I see the reflection of God in her loving eyes.

6

MOM, HE'S NOT WHO YOU Think (He Is

September 22, 1998

"Patience, patience," I mutter to myself, as I survey the hospital waiting room for signs of life. You'd think that after so many medical appointments, I would have mastered the art of waiting by now, especially by the age of forty-six. Expressionless faces stare into space. More resourceful patients pass the time by perusing old magazines. Even last year's bad news can be a welcome distraction from the troubling thoughts that invariably arise when facing a neurology appointment.

I shift in my seat, attempting to rearrange an aching body that has sat for too long. Soothing my unsettled mind will require more difficult maneuvers. It's hard not to focus on the tremors and lack of coordination that are now plaguing both of my hands. Will today's testing to investigate these symptoms finally determine the etiology of my illness and lead to a long overdue cure?

Stretching my legs, I rebalance the unfinished manuscript on my lap. So many pages of my disordered life stacked in such a neat pile. Yet the final chapter is yet to be written. I begin rereading chapter 5, hoping to distract myself by being transported back to a healthier time. I have managed to recapture so many memories of my life in this book. Why, then, is it so difficult to remember what it was like to be healthy? I can hardly imagine having the energy for a day filled with activity. Nor can I envision the freedom that comes from a healthy body functioning without complaint or resting quietly as the mind thinks deep thoughts. What must it be like to be freed from the burden of planning every movement in order to conserve each ounce of energy? Or to be spared the pain and suffering that inevitably result from even minimal activity?

A nurse brushes past me as she hurries into an examining room. She is seemingly oblivious to the throngs of patients waiting for her to summon them. All eyes look up expectantly for a moment, then resume their tiresome reading or blank staring as they attempt to hide their disappointment. Another chance to escape the patient ghetto has been lost. I force myself back to the manuscript.

"Dr. Rose . . ."

The sound of my name reverberates through the waiting room. I look up. A figure with a clipboard is scanning the area for a response. I struggle to rise, hoping to catch her eye before she concludes that I am a no-show.

"Dr. Rose?" she asks, scrutinizing me as I make my way toward her. Is she afraid I am an imposter who has become so tired of waiting that I have assumed a new identity just to escape the anonymity of the waiting room?

"Yes, I'm Beverly Rose." I smile confidently, trying to reassure her that she has indeed netted the right body. She appears convinced.

"Would you please follow me?" she requests.

I comply without a word. After being waylaid for so long in the oblivion of the waiting room, I would follow her anywhere. She leads me down a long hallway where a young physician motions me into the EMG lab.

"Let the tests begin," I mutter to myself with trepidation as I stretch out on the treatment table. This is not going to be easy for someone who is already in pain. After strapping electrodes to my right wrist, the doctor settles himself in front of the monitor for the first round of nerve-conduction studies.

Zap!

"Clench!" he shouts.

I curl my hand into a tight fist and gnash my teeth together.

"Good . . . Relax . . . Clench!"

The shocks come in rapid succession, sending my arm into spasms.

"Good. Now relax."

Relax? How can I relax when I am hooked up to a machine that is administering wave after wave of shocks? I struggle to distract myself from the assault. Meanwhile, the doctor is busy fiddling with dials and wires, seemingly oblivious to the pain he is inflicting upon my poor body. Finally he speaks to the corporeal appendage to his machine— me.

"Okay, I would also like to test your legs," he announces, almost with glee. Does he expect me to jump for joy at this proclamation? Or is he just trying to appear cheerful to cover up his guilt at perpetrating such torture upon such a nice person? I feel like saying, "No, thanks. As much as I would love to stay for more testing today, I really must go. You see, I've decided to move to the Bahamas, and the boat sails in five minutes. But, if you're ever in the neighborhood . . ." Instead, I reply with resignation, "Okay."

Nothing has ever been less okay in my life. Yet time and time again, I have opted to undergo painful medical tests in search of the elusive diagnosis that would finally explain why I fell victim to such a debilitating disease. Genetics. That is where the mystery probably lies. But how and why?

Meanwhile, electrodes are being moved from my wrists to my ankles and legs for more punishment. *Zap!* Another round of shocks. Shooting pain darts down my leg from the site of the blow just behind my knee. The appendage jerks as I attempt to distract myself. My mind screams all the way to the dark past to speak to the luminaries of medicine: *Why couldn't you have developed the technology years ago to explain the illness that plagued Aunt Sophie and Grandma? You would have spared all of us so many years of pain and frustration.*

Could some genetic defect possibly have caused such a devastating illness to be passed down through the generations? My mind wanders further as it struggles to escape the reality of the next assault. I become lost in reverie . . .

"No one knew at the time, Beverly. In those days, they just accepted it and lived with it."

"Mom, you're back?"

"Did you think I had left? You should know by now that I am always with you. Where else would a good Jewish mother be?"

"You are with me even in the confines of this awful EMG lab? That's dedication!"

"Why is that so hard to believe? Weren't you there with me in the ICU after my heart surgery? I felt so sorry for you.

You and your father traveled such a long distance just to see me every day, only to wait hour after hour for the few brief periods when they allowed visitors. You were so exhausted from your illness that you had to lie down in the backseat of the car throughout the day just to summon the energy to come back to the ICU. I told you and your father to go home. But you both refused. You spent every possible minute with me. So why wouldn't I do the same for my favorite daughter?"

"Your only daughter, Mom."

"My one and only!"

"But my being by your side before your death was different. That was a critical time for you. Besides, neither of us was dead . . . that is . . . until you finally succumbed. Yet here you are . . . somehow alive again."

"As long as you remember me, Beverly, I'll never die."

"Then you will live for eternity, Mom."

"And so will you, Beverly."

"I know, Mom. The rabbi has assured me of that."

"Oh yes, the rabbi. So, how is this mysterious friend of yours?"

"He is always fine, Mom. Well, even better than fine. You see, he doesn't have to worry about illness. In fact, you might say he specializes in healing."

"Oh, that's very interesting. Is he also a doctor?" Her excitement is nothing short of electrifying. Oh no. With all these electrodes attached to my body, any additional

electricity could fry me to a crisp! I quickly attempt to explain him to her before it's too late.

"He's not a doctor, Mom. But he is a healer."

"Do you mean he practices holistic medicine?"

"Sort of . . . but the original kind."

"Oh. He must be a real visionary."

"Very much so. Actually, I was hoping to tell you . . . I mean . . . He is not who you think he is."

"So, who is?"

"That's true. But, I mean . . . he's not of this world."

"Neither was your father when I met him. He was just like a Prince Charming coming to rescue me. Funny what love does to people."

"No, actually the rabbi is out of this world."

"That's wonderful. I can tell that you are crazy about him."

"No. I mean . . ."

"Dr. Rose?"

"Mom, since when did you become so formal?"

"Dr. Rose . . . the test is over."

I open my eyes. Electrodes are being removed from my legs. The doctor motions me to rise from the table. Bleary eyed and weak from pain, I take his hand and attempt to stand. Leaning on him for support, I steady myself and make my way toward the door.

Bidding him an enthusiastic good-bye, I limp into the hallway. "The test is over," I mutter to myself, "but not the trials."

7

NEVER
Again

July 1, 1957

"Sit down—all of you. Now!" the heavyset bus driver screams at the top of his lungs.

The rambunctious teenagers shove and squash, push and prod each other with abandon. No one is listening. After all, this isn't a real school bus. It is a transport vehicle taking us to camp. That means no rules—and certainly, no listening to adults.

"I mean it! I'll stop this bus right now if you don't all just sit down!" This guy is really getting mad.

We eye each other, wondering who will be the first wimp to fold under the pressure and take a seat.

"Okay, that's it!"

The rickety school bus comes to a screeching halt. Pimply faces and scrawny bodies lunge forward, falling one upon the other down the center aisle like dominoes.

"Now, listen up. This is just too dangerous. Either you all sit down right now and behave, or I'll turn this bus around and go home." This threat is too much for the unruly mob that has waited all year to escape from home to the mountains of Upstate New York.

One by one, the bodies begin to peel themselves off each other and dive into the empty seats as if escaping from a grenade. They have lost the battle . . . but not the war.

"Okay. That's better." The overweight torso of the temporarily victorious bus driver wedges itself back into its seat for another attempt at the road.

I sit motionless among this throbbing crowd of adolescents. It is my first time away from home, and it isn't going well so far. Who are these boisterous creatures? Certainly not the same well-mannered honor students I knew back home. I thought Jewish kids were supposed to be passive and well behaved—especially those who are so dedicated to Judaism that they have enrolled in a Zionist camp for the summer. Can they possibly be Jews? A moment of doubt comes over me. Maybe I boarded the wrong bus, and we're headed for Attica! But they certainly appear to be Jews. Look at them, sporting the shiny Star of David around their skinny necks and the camp logo on T-shirts hanging loosely from their underdeveloped bodies. Definitely Jews, I confirm. But, rebellious Jews? What an intriguing thought.

The bus grinds to a stop as the final destination looms in the distance. The occupants immediately jump out of their seats and race to the door.

"Hold it, kids! Hold it!" the bus driver barks. Using his huge belly as a battering ram, he plows through the skinny bodies, scattering them like toothpicks as he makes his way out of the bus. A tall, lanky collegiate young man with a khaki hat, small clipboard, and serious expression motions to the driver as he approaches. This must be the new "zookeeper."

We are unloaded unceremoniously like cargo reaching the final port after a long haul. The bus driver reclaims his bus with gusto. He speeds off in a huff, sand flying, fumes spewing into the air. He is obviously relieved to be rid of us.

I peruse the site for the first time. The camp is nestled in an impressive mountain valley. Crude wooden buildings dot the landscape. A makeshift sign hangs overhead announcing the camp name. "Hmmm, this is certainly no resort in the Catskills," I mutter to myself. No one else seems to take note of the fact that our summer home for the next month may be the most nondescript place on the face of the earth.

Suddenly, with no fanfare or explanation, we are herded into our cabins. Twelve bodies fill each bunkhouse, regardless of compatibility or similarity of background. I hear a lot of twanging as I enter the sparsely furnished structure. The inmates appear to be from the South, providing me with my first exposure to people from another region of America.

As I sit on the hard surface that has been designated my bed, my curiosity turns to amusement as several southern belles scamper over the floorboards, unloading hair dryers and hairpins, curlers, and countless other beauty items, no doubt picked up at some Miss Teenage America contest. Are they seriously planning to primp and preen all day in the midst of this spartan Zionist camp? By the time we are summoned for dinner, the place looks like a bungalow at a tropical resort, the girls are bedecked in finery, and I am fully expecting to walk out the door into a Hawaiian luau.

No such luck. Our counselor leads us to an unpretentious building marked DINING HALL to distinguish it from every other indistinguishable structure. We climb the steps and are greeted by an unkempt woman wearing a stained, white apron. She has obviously been working hard and is sweating profusely. I look around at my southern bunkmates and wonder what they think of this real live "before" picture.

"If you could all just take a seat around the tables," she directs with a stern expression.

We each find the nearest uncomfortable wooden chair and sit.

"This is the dining room where you will eat your meals. You will also work here, rotating through cooking, serving, and cleaning. Here we don't just receive. We give back."

I am not so sure I like the sound of this. At our house, Mom performs the majority of the kitchen duties. My greatest contribution is setting the table when asked, for which I am always generously showered with gratitude for my efforts. I look around at my bunkmates, who remain expressionless, appearing to be off in another world. Are they taking this all in or just waiting for the "floor show" to begin? Our hostess continues.

"There are prayers before and after each meal."

Sheets containing Hebrew words with English transliteration are passed around the table. I begin reading the unintelligible phrases. Out of the corner of my eye, I notice a stream of campers in white aprons carrying large trays of food. These are the first victims of the work schedule, I surmise. How did they manage to be pressed into service so quickly? I gain a new appreciation for my few remaining leisure moments that are destined to come to an end.

Before we begin eating, the dining hall erupts in song. I fumble for the song sheet, trying to follow the strange Hebrew prayer spelled out in English letters. Since I do not know the tune or the lyrics, this proves to be next to impossible. It will get easier, I hope, wondering how I ever managed to get myself into this.

And yet, somehow, sitting here in this barely identifiable structure, surrounded by strangers singing unintelligible phrases, there is a feeling of camaraderie. For this brief moment in time, as our bodies sway in unison to the tempo of the prayer, we transcend our ascetic surroundings and enter a world of boundless beauty. It is a place beyond places, where we as human beings find common ground in our vulnerabilities and deep desire for the love of a higher power. Regional differences and bodily adornments are stripped away as we stand naked before God to thank him for the sustenance we are about to receive . . . and are reminded that he alone is the provider of all things.

As the refrains cease, peace descends upon the hall. The previously unruly adolescents, who could hardly contain themselves on a moving bus, remain respectfully motionless, moved to silence. Gradually the room regains momentum as the clatter of dining activity resumes. Once the meal ends, the adolescent roar of feeding behaviors ceases again for the after-dinner prayers.

We traipse out of the dining hall, our stomachs filled to capacity. It has been a hearty kosher meal of soup, chicken, and vegetables. The July sun has made its way farther across the sky, hovering just above the western mountains. We return to our cabins to settle in.

As I sink into the pillow at an uncomfortably early hour, I ponder the events of the day. It has been a mixture of initial disappointment and surprising discovery. I can still hear the sweet refrains of the lyrical prayers and see the golden reflection of the descending summer sun shimmering on the freshly wiped tables. Maybe this place won't be so bad after all.

I am rudely awakened by the voice of our counselor. "Time to get up, girls," she pleads at too early an hour. The southern belles do not budge from their beauty sleep. "Come on. Rise and shine!" she shouts in a voice much too cheery for 6 A.M. Seeing no movement, she goes bed to bed, nudging the comatose bodies into consciousness. Yawns and protests greet her.

"Now? But it's so early," they whine.

There will be no negotiation. Our breakfast is waiting in the dining hall, having been prepared by some unfortunate group of campers who must have been aroused from a deep sleep in the dead of night. We have escaped this dreaded fate . . . for now. I arise to an unfamiliar scene of chaos and mayhem as late risers scurry about the cabin, frantically attempting to ready themselves for the morning meal.

After an adequate kosher breakfast, we begin our first day of classes. My schedule will include: History of the Jewish People, Beginning Hebrew, and Israeli Dancing. Pencils and spiral notebooks are distributed to each camper. The counselors are really serious about our education and expect us to take notes.

After several hours of classroom instruction, we are led into an impressive meeting hall for Israeli dancing. Large concentric circles are formed as the instructor slowly demonstrates each step of the first dance. The record player is turned on, and the spirited sounds of Israeli folk music electrify the air. We begin following her movements to the music, bumping into each other and stepping on the nearest shuffling feet. The instructor encourages us with great enthusiasm and optimism as we repeatedly turn in the wrong direction with the wrong leg at the wrong time. Over and over again, we attempt the complicated maneuvers.

Suddenly the spastic undulations give rise to rhythmic waves of motion. Each link falls in line within the chain of hands as we are pulled along effortlessly by a power greater than ourselves. Swirling through the air, barely holding on to the sweaty hand clasped in mine, I am carried to new heights. The building is pulsating as a hundred pairs of feet stamp in unison, causing rhythmic vibrations that seem to reverberate through time.

By the power of our bodies and the intensity of our effort, we have recaptured the fervor of the Israeli pioneers who danced to this impassioned music as they established the state of Israel. With callused hands and aching muscles, they joined together to dance this very dance, after toiling all day to turn the arid, foreboding desert into a "land of milk and honey." We are the inheritors of their struggle . . . and their spirit.

As I exit the meeting hall, I remember the excitement I felt as I prepared to leave for camp shortly after the Six Day War. What a twist of fate to be attending a Zionist camp in July 1967, just weeks after Israel's impressive victory. I remind myself of the reason I have chosen to come here. I am seeking the true meaning of my Jewish identity and knowledge of the country that is supposed to be my birthright, the state of Israel. This second day of camp life has more than fulfilled my expectations. But tomorrow will bring an even more dramatic turn of events. We are scheduled to spend several days deeply immersed in the history and meaning of the Holocaust.

It is with trepidation that I arise to greet this day. Rumors abound about the horrors we will see as we watch films and listen to stories about the shocking events of the Holocaust. A solemn mood pervades the cabin as we dress for breakfast.

After the morning meal, we head for the classroom. As we settle into our seats, we stare at a large movie screen that is suspended from the ceiling. Helpers lower the blinds as a counselor proceeds to the front of the room. His expression is serious, his tone unnervingly somber. "Today we begin our study of the Holocaust. You are all probably already aware of what happened during World War II under Hitler's regime, when six million Jews were exterminated. But we want to show you more than you have probably seen and teach you more than you may already know. This will not be easy for you. But it is necessary for you to understand as Jews, so that you know who you are and that you must work diligently to ensure that it can never happen again."

The lights dim as black-and-white images sprawl across the screen. Scenes of hate stain the air, strangely out of place in this peaceful, verdant valley of Upstate New York. The camera pans to reveal skin-and-bone near-corpses huddled in crude barracks. Outside, barbed wire encloses a muddy field, patrolled by SS troops and guard dogs. Dead prisoners hang from ropes in the distance, ignored by captors and captives alike. The inmates, hardly alive and barely clothed in filthy striped uniforms marked with the Star of David, seem too weak to weep anymore. The camera zooms in on large piles of trash. Closer inspection reveals a huge entanglement of eyeglasses from prisoners who can no longer see. These silent, wire-rimmed witnesses of clandestine atrocities will be refashioned by the Nazis and sold. Will the eyes of their new owners be willing to bear witness?

The sky is blackened by ashes spewing from the crematorium, which is systematically disposing of the evidence. The mangled bodies that have been transported from the gas chambers are loaded into ovens, one by one, soul by soul, and obliterated from the face of the earth. We are spared the stench . . . but not the stink. Bars of soap and lampshades come into view, seemingly innocuous items, until we are told that they have been made from human skin. I can no longer bear to watch, but I dare not turn away. Not like the world did.

Mercifully, the film ends, and we are returned to light . . . but not to life. A deathly pall pervades the room. Screams of the dead echo in the silence. I scan the faces of my fellow campers. They are frozen in shock and horror. Tears blur my eyes as a wave of nausea descends upon me. No one dares speak. No one *can* speak. The crimes are unspeakable. Yet one must be heard. I struggle to recoup my senses and verbalize, but I sink further downward. My mind is too numb to reengage. Even the most valiant effort to pose the question *why?* is squelched under the unbearable weight of agonizing sorrow.

We rise without a sound and depart. The summer day, which only hours before had been infused with light and life, appears void and sur-real. It is nuclear winter in July. A bomb has exploded in my soul. I am certain it will resonate throughout my being for the rest of my life. Radiation sickness eats at the bones forever. The nauseating feelings will return over and over again as I remember what I witnessed today. And yet I must remember. It is only by remembrance that this can never happen again. Never, ever again.

As I leave this scene of horrors, I ponder the ultimate question: Where was God? Or maybe, more fittingly: Where was humanity? If the Jews had possessed a homeland, would such mass murder have been unthinkable, impossible? Could this ever happen again, maybe even to me? How could it? Wouldn't I be spared such a shocking fate by the good graces of friends? I have no answers—just unsettling, agonizing questions.

Suddenly I become aware that I am clutching a single piece of paper that was stuffed into my hand upon leaving for break. Situating myself under the nearest tree, I begin to read:

> First they came for the communists,
> And I didn't speak up
> Because I was not a communist.
> Then they came for the trade unionists,
> And I didn't speak up
> Because I was not a trade unionist.
> Then they came for the Jews,
> And I didn't speak up
> Because I was not a Jew.
> Then they came for me,
> And there was no one left to speak for me.
> To make certain this doesn't happen again
> To anyone, anywhere,
> Injustice must be the concern of everyone, everywhere.
>
> —Adapted from a statement attributed to Pastor Martin
> Niemoller, a concentration-camp prisoner and leader of
> the Confessional Church, an anti-Nazi group that con-
> demned the regime's racial policies.

8

FAMILY
Business

December 24, 1968

"Jewish Pig!" The grotesque, porcine face on the gaudy storefront poster screams profanities at me. I hurry past the sign, avoiding eye contact with the Black Panther members gathered inside their headquarters. Any meeting of the eyes would only provoke further epithets. And when you can't see eye to eye, there can be no meeting of the minds. It is the late 1960s, and in this poor, volatile neighborhood that abuts the infamous section of Brooklyn known as Bedford Stuyvesant, the crescendo of racial tensions has climaxed. Any gesture, however inadvertent, can become an incendiary device, setting off a powder keg of emotions. It is an explosion that we can ill afford with our family store just next door to the Black Panthers' base of operations.

My father places his key into the lock as I catch up to him. The rusted iron gate, a meek guardian of the family livelihood, screeches open, compressing link by link like an old accordion being robbed of its very last breath. We will spend a stifling twelve hours here, dispensing Christmas presents to last-minute shoppers.

As my father rushes into the store to turn on the lights, my mother and Ed follow behind. They are engaged in an animated discussion, seemingly oblivious to the less-than-hospitable surroundings. Brushing by me, they make their way to the door through which masses of humanity will pass on this last shopping day before Christmas.

I stare up at the faint December sun, which is struggling to light the gray, polluted sky. The dim rays barely illuminate the cheap, tattered, red-and-green Christmas displays. These halfhearted attempts by predominately Jewish storekeepers fall on suspicious eyes in a community where outside merchants are unwanted and, in many cases, despised. It is an uneasy, sometimes dangerous, interplay. Local store-owners provide shoppers with an attractive alternative to long subway trips downtown. Customers are convinced that they pay dearly for this convenience to greedy white merchants who return to comfortable homes on Long Island.

Misunderstanding and misconceptions abound on both sides, leading to friction, harsh words, and sometimes, even murder. Recently an armed robbery claimed the life of an Italian merchant who owned the delicatessen on the next block. He was one of the kindest shopkeepers in the neighborhood. At age sixteen, I am already a veteran of years of anxious waiting and wondering whether my parents will return home from work in a car or a coffin. Today, however, should a robbery occur, I will be here to witness their fate . . . as well as my own.

"Beverly, are you coming in?" my mother shouts from the door in a worried tone.

"In a minute, Mom," I reply. I'd rather savor these few remaining moments perusing the neighborhood from the store lobby than begin the long, interminable hours of sales.

The streets are beginning to buzz with activity. Mothers are pushing strollers while groups of children compete for their hands and tug
at their skirts. It is heartbreaking to witness so many children vying for
so little. They settle for tattered hand-me-downs from more fortunate
siblings who were born first, and share meager meals that must be
apportioned to feed many mouths. Although parents struggle to provide sustenance, they can barely make ends meet. Many are on welfare,
which keeps the family barely afloat. I feel guilty taking their money for
clothing they so desperately need. And yet, I remind myself that, but
for this livelihood, my family might also be living in poverty—in a
ghetto called the Lower East Side.

"Lock the door behind you," my father shouts as I make my way
past the stream of shoppers entering the store.

I turn back and gently push the old, heavy door shut. The lock
grips tightly with a loud click. In reality, it is a system of false security,
for when the next customer arrives and presses the buzzer to be let in,
a robber could easily slip in from behind. I wonder what prompted my
parents to recently install this apparatus. Have things really gotten that
much worse? What haven't they told me? And how many more
Christmases will we have to spend as prisoners in our own store?

I survey my surroundings. Despite the constant influx of new children's and ladies' fashions that fill the display cases and shelves, it seems
that nothing really changes in this stale environment. The long, narrow
interior remains dingy, even under the glow of rows of fluorescent
lights. Old ladders rattle back and forth on rickety tracks along the
dilapidated walls like obsolete trolleys trapped in repetitious routes,
destined for nowhere. Dust hangs heavy in the air from years of accu-
mulated dirt and lint, creating a permanent material mist that dulls the

senses and fogs the brain. Cracked glass display cases, too expensive to replace, are held together with strips of yellowing Scotch tape. Along the walls, cubbyholes bulge with thousands of items to be sold in the endless hours ahead. "Shelve one more day into oblivion," I mutter as I think of my high school friends in suburbia who will spend this day socializing in a safer, saner place.

"Beverly, we could use your help," my father calls from across the aisle.

"Okay, Dad," I reply, although it really isn't. But I have no choice. And neither does he.

With no family support for college or training, my parents were compelled to start from scratch, beginning with my father selling undershirts door to door. Eventually they worked their way up to renting increasingly larger stores. Yet despite many years of hard labor, they can only afford the overhead in a poor neighborhood such as this. It is an honest living, however, that pays the low-interest mortgage on a modest suburban house, courtesy of the GI Bill, and gives my brother and me a chance to grow up far from the congestion and crime of the city. That is, except on Saturdays and holidays, when we accompany our parents to supply the additional sales help they cannot afford to pay "real" salespeople. Having worked for my father since the age of ten, however, I probably qualify to join the union by now.

With all the energy I can muster, I plunge into the crowd to scout out my first customer. The throngs of shoppers give way as I weave through the narrow aisles in search of my prey. Suddenly I am cut off at the pass and crash into a large, stationary body. The irresistible force has met the immovable object.

"May I help you?" I ask as I attempt to regain my balance . . . and my senses. I try to appear pleasant, if not interested.

"I'm looking for a girdle," the overweight customer with the bulging posterior states resolutely.

I try to maintain a straight face as I dread the next few moments of my young salesperson's life. I search the usual spot for the boxes of corsets but find baby buntings instead.

"Uh . . . Dad!" I scream.

My father is somewhere in the back storeroom, which means he might as well be in New Jersey. Nevertheless, I persist.

"Where are the girdles?" I yell interstate. He is always moving items around due to seasonal demands and space limitations, and I have learned to ask, rather than attempt to search further on my own.

"In the front to the right," he yells.

The thrill of actually receiving a response on the first try is eclipsed by the enigmatic nature of the message. There are hundreds of items in the front of the store, and "on the right" depends upon which way you are facing at the time.

Luckily, my mother rescues me from my quandary. "In the blue boxes on the bottom shelf in front of you, dear," she says softly as she emerges from behind the crowd. "Do you want me to show you?" She is always watching out for me, trying to make my life easier.

"No, thanks, Mom. I see them."

I am extremely grateful. A long girdle hunt has been mercifully averted. Now I desperately wish she could rescue me from this sale. She would patiently, with great care and compassion, bring this eager customer through the vast landscape of girdles and their innumerable attributes. But Mom is already waiting on several people.

So I must step forward and courageously place my body in the line of fire.

As I proceed to the counter, the customer follows, waddling down the narrow aisle, squeezing in between counters, which tip slightly to make way for the heavy cargo. She settles herself in front of the display case in eager anticipation of the corset that will transform her from Kate Smith into Marilyn Monroe.

"Uh, what size are you looking for?" I ask. Meanwhile, I scan the boxes, searching for the one with the most Xs, denoting how extra, extra large the garment is.

"Size 3X," she replies.

She's going to need more Xs than that, I tell myself but make no comment. I doubt girdles come with more Xs. Grabbing the Maidenform box, I place it on the counter and open it. Out pops a lacy, elastic mass rolled up in tissue paper. I gingerly unwrap it and stretch the garment out in front of her. So little material . . . so much to accomplish.

She picks up the corset and, stretching it over her waist, seems satisfied. "I'll take it," she says decidedly, handing it back to me.

I whisk the garment from her hands before she can change her mind, and race to the counter to ring up the sale. Smiling, and for the first time meaning it, I place the girdle in a bag, take the cash, and thank her profusely. As she wobbles out of the store, I realize how grateful I am that I don't have to follow her home to witness the pinching and prodding, squeezing and squirming it will take to get all the necessary parts properly placed within that poor 3X girdle—sort of like doing the limbo . . . only standing up. Having satisfied my corpulent customer, I am filled with a sense of accomplishment. Not bad. My first sale of the day. Now only a thousand or so to go!

I glance over at Carrie, our "salesgirl," who is gray-haired and in her sixties—far more a grandma than a girl. She is busy selling polo shirts as she chats casually with a customer. Carrie is usually oblivious to the teeming throngs who increasingly demand her attention. She is her own person, working slowly and steadily, regardless of the day or the circumstances. It is hard to know whether this is her style or the result of an underlying determination not to be controlled by any-one—whether boss or customer. She is in the unenviable position of being a black woman working for a white Jewish merchant in a pre-dominately black neighborhood. To further complicate matters, her daughter frequents the Black Panthers headquarters next door. Carrie, who is clearly a Black Panther sympathizer, tolerates accusations of being an "Uncle Tom" because of her need to place economics above politics.

Our relations with Carrie are generally pleasant but strained. She was the deciding factor in my father's refusal to allow the FBI to use our store as a base of operations to bug the neighboring Black Panthers organization. Under Carrie's scrutiny, there was bound to be a leak, and the ramifications could be deadly for us. "I have a family to protect," my father had pleaded with the unsympathetic G-men, who applied constant pressure, nevertheless. Finally they gave up, grudgingly accepting this "unpatriotic" response. They had to. After all, we do not live in a police state.

Countless protest marchers believe otherwise, however. This neigh-borhood has been rocked by the ongoing social and racial tensions that have plagued the country throughout most of the 1960s. Besides the deaths of thousands of American soldiers in the increasingly unpopular Vietnam War, we have seen young leaders fall while passionately promoting the cause of peace. First there was the assassination of President John F. Kennedy, followed by the murders of Martin Luther King Jr. and Robert Kennedy. We are still recovering from the riots that broke out after Dr. King's death in April. I remember the sinking feeling I had when I saw the news flash: "Martin Luther King Jr. shot in Memphis." It seemed that all the advocates of peace, who preached love and nonviolence, would be felled by a war of hate.

My father closed the store the next day out of respect . . . and fear. He sensed that the heightened tensions would reach a boiling point, erupting in violence in the streets. He was right. Rioters invaded the neighborhood, trashing and plundering numerous shops. They backed trucks up to storefronts and tied heavy steel chains around the protective iron gates. With a push of the accelerator, they tore twisted metal from its tracks. Once inside, scores of looters rushed in to grab every item in sight.

We waited anxiously at home for the dreaded phone call from the Brooklyn police breaking the news to my parents that their livelihood had been destroyed. But no call came. My father returned to find his store intact. Liquor and appliance storeowners had not been so lucky. It seems the rioters had engaged in systematic robbery rather than uncontrollable expressions of grief, carefully choosing the most valuable targets for looting. "Selective rioting," my father muttered as he surveyed the streets with disdain . . . but relief.

These outbreaks of violence do little to defuse the smoldering resentment in the hearts of those blacks who wish to force Jewish merchants out of the neighborhood. Their anger puzzles me, for both groups have much in common. Throughout history, Jews have also been a disenfranchised, impoverished, and persecuted minority. In fact, such commonalities have spurred fervent support of the civil rights movement by a significant number of Jews. So why do the Black Panthers aim hateful anti-Semitic posters and inflammatory rhetoric at a group that is, for the most part, sympathetic to their cause?

Even in the shadow of all this racial tension, we, as human beings, do manage to connect. I always marvel at my mother's compassion and understanding. In the midst of all this conflict, she spends warm and caring interludes with customers, regardless of race or politics. She always takes time to inquire about their families while expertly assisting them in selecting the perfect gift. I surmise that it is bitter memories of childhood deprivation—as well as her kind and loving spirit—that fuel her determination to reach out to all people who are less fortunate. I am certain that her intelligence enables her to perceive cultural differences keenly. Yet she always manages to find the similarities of the heart.

"Beverly, are you hungry?" my mother inquires.

"Yes, I guess so," I answer. I have been so busy waiting on customers that I've hardly had time to notice my hunger pains.

She leads me to the back of the store where a sandwich awaits. The flow of customers has slowed somewhat, allowing us to spend a few minutes together.

"Beverly, there is something I haven't told you because I knew how upsetting it would be for you."

Suddenly I have lost my appetite.

"Really? What is it?" I say, not really wanting to know.

"You may be wondering why we recently installed the buzzer system."

"Yes, I thought it was strange that you placed an automatic lock on the door after all these years."

"Well, we had an incident several months ago," she continues. "Two men came in with shotguns . . ."

As she describes the horrendous events of the armed robbery, I cannot contain myself. I break down in tears. It is my worst nightmare come true. My mother comforts me, but to no avail.

Trying to compose myself, I return to the sales floor. After the flurry of final purchases, my father locks the door behind the last customer, and the Christmas season is over for us. My Uncle Irv, who has come to join us this evening for the last round of patrons, retrieves an empty shoebox from under the counter and begins to stuff it full of bills—the day's revenue. He will place this makeshift "safe" under his arm and nonchalantly stroll to our car, eyes darting nervously from side to side, hoping no one will notice the ruse. It is the most anxious time of the day, when we dread the possible mugging that would deprive us of all the earnings from the most profitable day of the year. Yet somehow he always manages to safeguard the precious cargo and make it to the car. That's my Uncle Irv—a poor man's Brinks Service.

We are released into the night like pinched and ruffled pigeons escaping from a mercilessly tiny coop. The icy air awakens our senses, enlivens our limbs, and lifts our sagging spirits. The streets are quiet now. Shoppers have long since headed home for last-minute Christmas preparations. For them, tomorrow will bring a once-a-year bonanza of surprises as the wrapping paper and bows we so meticulously fashioned will be torn from brightly colored boxes and strewn over furniture and floors in the merriment of Christmas morning. We, however, will sleep late and awaken exhausted . . . but relieved.

I join my mother in the backseat of the car and settle in for the long drive to the suburbs. As we travel the nearly empty streets, I focus on the Christmas decorations that are suspended high overhead, strung from lamppost to lamppost. Reflections of red-and-green stars and bells dance on the front windshield, creating splashes of Christmas color. Once on the Belt Parkway, the night is devoid of all Christmas reminders. I close my eyes in weary rest . . .

"Put your hands up or I'll shoot!" the big, burly intruder demands, pointing a rifle directly at her head. "You, too," he yells, waving the rifle in front of the storekeeper's face. "Now, step slowly to the register and give me all the money."

The white faces of the storeowners blanch, accentuating even more the difference between them and their assailants.

"Step aside, step aside," the accomplice screams as the frightened shoppers take refuge behind the counters.

"The money, man, the money!" the gunman prods. "NOW!"

The storekeeper rushes to the cash register, popping open the drawer, fingers scrambling for the bills. With trembling hands, he piles the cash on the counter and retreats.

"That's all you have? Come on, man. I know you have more than that," the robber sneers. "You Jews always keep more than that. Where's the rest? Hiding it in a box somewhere?"

"No, I don't have any more. That's all I have. It's been a slow day."

"Sure," the gunman mutters with contempt, waving the rifle with an even more threatening gesture.

"Please, mister. Please don't shoot," the trembling woman pleads. "I have two children at home." Her eyes fill with fright and tears.

"Shut up, lady!" He picks up the cash from the counter and shoves the rifle under her nose.

There is a pause that lasts an eternity. No one dares move . . . or breathe. Finally, the robber waves his hand in disgust. "Let's get out of here," he yells to his partner in crime.

Keeping their rifles aimed at the victims' heads, the gunmen back out of the door and vanish into the crowded street. The customers scurry out of the store, leaving the shaken shopkeepers behind. The merchant's wife runs to the door to make certain the robbers are gone before calling the police. Her husband retreats to the basement to retrieve the box of cash he has hidden there. He opens it with a sigh of relief. It contains most of the day's take. In reality, the gunmen have stolen very little of the earnings.

"Are you all right?" he inquires of his motionless wife as he shows her the box.

She stares at him with a tortured expression as she pictures her two children receiving a phone call from the Brooklyn police informing them that their parents would not be coming home tonight . . . or any other night, ever again. Just like her mother, her beloved children, Edward and Beverly, would have become orphans.

I awaken in a cold sweat as the car lurches forward. I search my mother's face for reassuring signs of life. She sits in an exhausted stupor, eyes fixed forward, daydreaming. Her countenance is expressionless now—the same face that stared in terror down the barrel of a rifle, pleading for her life . . . and ours. I gaze at her motionless figure in the shadows and wonder why my parents' lives were not taken that day. Was it my mother's courageous, selfless plea to spare her life for the sake of her children? Or was it the love of a higher power who mercifully intervened, just in time, saving this family from the ultimate of tragedies? I will never know.

As we arrive at our driveway, I ponder the meaning of Christmas. I wonder where God will be on Christmas morning as those ghetto children whose parents could not afford to buy them presents go empty-handed while other more fortunate youngsters receive armfuls of toys. Can the gifts we sold today really honor the Christian God, much less give birth to the brotherhood he so passionately preached? I yearn to understand but, from my vantage point, cannot. Yet, of this I am certain. We, who are not Christian, have been granted the greatest present of all this Christmas Eve. For we have survived. And through this gift of life, we can join with our Christian counterparts in expressing gratitude to the God who gives life.

"Thank God we made it through another Christmas," my father exclaims with a sigh of relief as he unlocks our front door with renewed fervor. Truer words were never spoken.

9

I AM MY
Brother's Keeper

"Watch your step, madam," he cautions. The bleary-eyed tourist places her hand firmly on the railing and disembarks from the bus. "Let's move along now," the youthful tour guide urges as he motions to the next sightseer in an attempt to hurry her out of the bus. Tugging at her arm, he pulls her down the stairs onto the hallowed soil. "Next," he says in an uninspired tone.

We have been on the road since 8 A.M., touring the holy sites of Jerusalem. We visited the old city, winding through the Jaffa Gate to the Christian Quarter. We viewed the Holy Sepulchre, the Western Wall, Mount Zion, and the Mount of Olives. We have two last stops, and the guide is eager to get on with it. For him, these holy sites evoke little emotion. They are part of a familiar, everyday landscape. Besides, he tours these sacred shrines every day. And this is just another work-day. For me, however, as a nineteen-year-old avid supporter of the state of Israel, this is the opportunity of a lifetime.

The tourists file out of the bus, cameras dangling from their necks, like hunters on safari waiting to shoot their next prey. Images captured, they will return home to envious friends and neighbors, displaying these trophies with pride and embellished stories. I glance at my brother as we reach the front of the bus. He is adjusting the lens on the movie camera, which mysteriously stopped functioning yesterday at the Dead Sea. Apparently one must expect such things when entering a region with such an inauspicious name.

The tour guide takes my hand and yanks me out of the bus. I am the last one to disembark, much to his relief . . . and mine. For Ed and I had been in the unenviable position of sitting in the very last row of the tour bus, directly in front of a vibrating, rattling, spitting air conditioner. This was purely a matter of inexperience. Other, more seasoned tourists avoided such a fate by coming early to fill the front seats first. To make matters worse, the deafening noise level of the antiquated air conditioner was inversely proportionate to its output. I turn to Ed, who is vigorously rubbing his ears, trying to revive them.

"Wasn't that air conditioner loud?" I inquire.

"What?" he shouts. Question asked and answered. I make a mental note to race back to the bus early for departure to avoid further hearing loss.

I attempt to engage my brother once again. Hoping to recapture the thrill of finally being here in the land of Israel, I exclaim with great enthusiasm, "Isn't it amazing how we can feel so at home in a country so far away?"

"Yeah," he answers, "sort of like being in Brooklyn."

That wasn't exactly what I had in mind, but I make no reply. At least he hasn't turned a deaf ear.

We have been touring Europe for the past month together and have actually managed to keep fairly good relations. My brother is generally great company for sightseeing. Before our excursion, he expertly planned our itinerary, studying all the essential facts about each of the countries we intended to visit. His efforts were particularly impressive since we had so little time to prepare. We had no idea that the summer of 1971 would usher in the lowest airfares to London in recent memory—a mere two hundred dollars round trip. What better way to spend the little money we saved toiling in my father's store than to travel abroad, visiting London, Amsterdam, Paris, Rome, and Israel. What we hadn't anticipated, however, was that every college student in America would have the same idea.

Once on European soil, we faced the monumental task of finding a place to stay. Our first night in a London youth hostel did not go well. Makeshift beds were set up in a gymnasium. The unsavory and bedraggled guests who roamed the halls looked like recently released prisoners from the Tower of London. I spent a sleepless night cradling my purse under my pillow.

The next morning we combed London for inexpensive private accommodations. We dialed countless numbers, finally finding a nearby room to rent. A conservatively dressed lady answered the door, and we made our way into what appeared to be a house converted into a hotel. Eyeing us suspiciously, she explained in a not-so-friendly tone that she had only one room left—and it was in the attic. We eagerly accepted. The alternative was returning to prison camp. She led us up flight after flight of stairs, which ended in a narrow series of crude, wooden rungs. Finally, huffing and puffing, we made it to hotel heaven. It was tiny but adequate. There were separate beds, running water, and a toilet. And I didn't have to sleep on my purse.

Actually, it was a godsend that was almost revoked. For my brother, who is meticulously clean about his wardrobe, had decided to wash his underwear one morning before we left for the day. As I waited downstairs for him to come to breakfast, he had made a makeshift clothesline and strung his BVDs and other unmentionables all across the attic rafters. When we returned to the hotel that evening, we were accosted by the infuriated, proper British hostess who had seen one jockstrap too many.

It was a brutal interrogation. "You are brother and sister?" she asked in an accusing tone, certain that we were, in reality, shacking up, thereby turning her dignified hotel into a red-light district. My brother and I retreated to the attic and proceeded to argue it out. He was indignant and intransigent. "I had to do my laundry" was his defense. Knowing how difficult it was to rent a room in London, I retorted, "Great! I'm sure the homeless people who share our cardboard box will be very appreciative."

As I remember the incident, I can't help looking over at my brother and smiling. He is an extraordinarily intelligent, learned individual who has earned all sorts of academic accolades. Too bad he failed in underwear etiquette.

"Beverly, pay attention! We'll lose our place in line," Ed urges, nudging me toward the building. As the line slowly moves, our traveling companions chatter to fill the time. Happy to be out of the sweltering tour bus—and out of earshot of the guide—they ventilate.

"When are we going to eat again? It's been two and a half hours since lunch. Don't they feed you on this tour?"

"Doesn't he talk too fast? Why doesn't he slow down? I can hardly understand him with that accent."

"They have the most sophisticated army in the world. So how come they can't make a bus with a better air conditioner?"

"Do you think I got a bargain buying that wooden camel for two dollars from that poor Arab boy? Maybe if I had waited, I could have bought it later at the Arab market for a dollar."

"Can't they make this line go faster? How long are they going to keep us waiting here in the hot sun? I'm going to melt."

Standing in the shadow of Yad Vashem, Israel's memorial to the victims of the Holocaust, these questions seem absurdly out of place.

Finally we enter the low-lying structure. Immediately we are engulfed in blackness. My eyes squint as they labor to accommodate to the scene. It is a futile attempt. There is no way to become accustomed to this sight. A flame thrusts glowing pulses into the darkness but can shed little light upon the carved letters etched into the black floor: AUSCHWITZ, DACHAU, . . . Names of Nazi concentration camps are indelibly imprinted in stone. Ashes of victims buried in the crypt near the flickering flame scream from the grave. We stand in profound silence. Murmurs emanate from the darkness. "Yit-gadal, v'yit-kadash sh'may raba . . ." The Mourner's Prayer reverberates in muffled echoes as the soft sobbing of onlookers creates a mournful accompaniment to the plaintive cries. Suddenly a shriek pierces the air as a woman, crying hysterically, claws her way through the crowd, escaping out the door. Could she be a survivor of the death camps?

My eyes fill with tears as I stare at the searing flame. In the light, I see the silhouette of a face. His countenance gains intensity in the fiery glow, begging me to remember our strange encounter in Amsterdam just weeks before. I can still see him sitting in the shadows . . .

"Excuse me. May I ask you a question?"

No reply. He barely stirs.

"Excuse me," Ed repeats.

The young Dutchman, seated against the far wall, nods. His eyes are sullen, almost grief stricken.

"We are American tourists. We were walking along and saw this building. It didn't seem to have any markings. But then we noticed a small Jewish star under the eave. Is this a temple?"

He nods again, his eyes staring past us. We inch closer to him.

"We thought it was a little strange to see this lone building in the midst of all these highways."

The ghostly figure breaks his silence, speaking in hushed tones. "This was a very active synagogue in a large Jewish neighborhood. Then, one day, the Nazis came during a High Holy Day service and arrested everyone. Afterward they leveled the entire neighborhood with bulldozers and built highways to cover the streets where the homes of the congregants once stood."

I wonder why the Nazis hadn't also destroyed this temple. But I dare not ask.

"Very few Jews remain. I am the rabbi here . . ."

The rabbi of a synagogue comprised mostly of the dearly departed, *I think to myself. I stare at the mournful eyes, which have been condemned to relive horrifying scenes of a past that transcends time.*

The room is eerily silent. Empty rows of seats evoke visions of better days. Once, this synagogue was overflowing with eager congregants whose lives were filled with hope and promise.

Their images overtake my mind as they find their places for the Yom Kippur service. I imagine myself seated in the back row. My mother is at my side, singing familiar prayers. Ed joins in as he fingers his tallith in rhythm. My father scans the room with a bored expression, wondering when the service will end. Suddenly storm troopers violate the sanctity of the sanctuary. Their boots pound mercilessly on the hard, wooden floors, sending shock waves throughout the congregation. One by one, screaming, terrified worshipers are dragged out of the synagogue. The invaders seize my father, then my brother, and reach for my mother . . .

A hand grabs my arm. *I struggle to free myself from the Nazi who is about to drag me away to my death.*

"Come on, Beverly. Let's go," my brother urges, continuing to tug at my arm. *I recoil, refusing to succumb to my fate.*

"Beverly!" my brother shouts. "Get a grip! It's time to move on."

The blood drains from my face. A bone-chilling thought pierces my consciousness. If we had been sitting in that temple just thirty years ago . . .

Ed pulls me into the next room, bringing me face to face with a reality I can hardly bear. Photographs and documents line the walls, chronicling the morbid details of Hitler's "final solution to the Jewish problem." Images of tortured faces and mangled bodies stand accusing, daring the world for answers. Always, the haunting question, "Why?"

Once outside, the fresh air does little to revive my spirit. Familiar feelings of despair wash over me. I am flooded by the same unsettling emotions that plagued me at camp during those grueling days of study about the Holocaust. That experience left me feeling alone as a Jew in a world of uncaring Gentiles who only grudgingly accept my presence and periodically even seek to eradicate my people from the face of the earth. Was this really the intended message of my impassioned Zionist counselors, who were admonishing a new generation to never forget? I don't know. Many of my ancestors were murdered in horrid pogroms. My family has been victimized by vicious anti-Semitic slurs in Brooklyn. We were lucky to escape the ravages of the Holocaust, although we still suffer from its brutal effects on our consciousness. Maybe the whole world is against us. Could it be that this is why I was encouraged to have primarily Jewish friends? My father once told me that every non-Jew is an anti-Semite deep down inside. It is a horrifying thought.

I ponder these troubling questions as we walk along a treelined path. Out of the corner of my eye, I notice that in front of each tree is a plaque. I question my brother, who has stopped to read one of the inscriptions.

"This must be the Avenue of the Righteous Among the Nations," he concludes.

I stare at him, perplexed. I have never heard of this site.

He continues, "These trees have been planted in honor of the non-Jews who risked their lives to save Jews during the Holocaust. The plaques list names of righteous Gentiles and their country of residence during the war. I think I once read that these heroes actually planted the trees themselves. When Israel passed a law to establish Yad Vashem to perpetuate the memory of the Jewish Holocaust victims, the legislators included a stipulation that these righteous Gentiles also be honored. A commission was formed to review cases on an ongoing basis, in order to award this honor to deserving candidates."

As we pass by tree after tree, I am stunned at the sheer number of plaques and awed at the nobility of such brave acts. These people were indeed heroes, risking not only their own lives, but sometimes even the lives of their families to help people they may not have even known. They faced imprisonment in concentration camps and probable death. There is no way to comprehend fully the extent of their selflessness. These non-Jews were the true embodiment of the Good Samaritan.

We walk back to the tour bus in silence, attempting to grasp the enormity of what we have just witnessed. Our traveling companions are milling around aimlessly as they wait for the tour guide. No rush to grab the best seats now to get a better view of the sights. They have already seen too much.

I wander over to a statue and read the inscription at the base of the biblical figure. With no one around to hear me, I whisper to the tortured stone face, "Why is there so much suffering in this world?" The mute figure speaks to me in thought: *We cannot know. But be assured. God does exist.* "I know, Job," I answer silently. "He created you and me . . . along with the righteous Gentiles."

10

HE WILL *NEVER*
Let Me Down

October 6, 1998

"One must have the patience of Job," I mutter as I attempt to coax myself from bed. Yesterday's collaboration with my editor has left me feeling exhausted and in pain. Today minimal tasks will become even more challenging than usual. Nevertheless, I must rise to the challenge and summon the energy, if not the enthusiasm, for the activities of daily living.

It is late morning. The mail carrier is departing from the parking lot, having dutifully delivered today's assortment of junk mail and bills. Hundreds of expectant residents anxiously await these treasures, nevertheless. Someday I'll witness one of my elderly neighbors leap for joy—right out of her wheelchair—as she discovers a check for ten million dollars from some magazine clearinghouse. What a way to go!

I make my way slowly to the mailbox, not expecting to receive such life-altering news. Thumbing through the stack, I pull out a letter from one of my doctors. My hopes rise as I tear open the envelope and begin to read. But, once again, no news is bad news. The doctor writes that he is still unable to determine a definitive diagnosis and is in favor of my suggestion that I arrange a workup with the top-notch Muscular Dystrophy Association researcher from New York whom I recently contacted. The letter concludes, "I would be most interested in any further thoughts that he has with some of the newer techniques . . . his laboratory is one of the absolutely finest in the world for looking at some of the unusual muscular problems. There is no doubt in my mind that there are certain keys that we have not identified to unlock a few doors in the field of muscle energy metabolism. Our facility is not equipped to do the basic research necessary for this. . . . Feel free to call if I can be of further help."

The sincerity of his words and his concern for my welfare are touching. But I dread undergoing more painful medical workups that may not even lead to an answer.

When will it end, Lord? When will it end?

The red light on my WebTV unit signals that I have received e-mail. It has been months since I first contacted the MDA researcher from New York, and weeks since he began analysis on the preserved muscle tissue from my 1992 biopsy that was recently sent to him from Boston. Could this be the result for which I have been waiting so long?

I quickly retrieve my messages. The researcher's words fill the screen: ". . . the stain for cytochrome c oxidase [COX] was abnormally reduced. Although, given the extremely small size of the needle biopsy, we could only measure two enzyme activities, we did confirm a decrease of COX. So you may, in fact, have a mitochondrial dysfunction. . . ."

I stare at the medical terminology, struggling to grasp the enormity of this statement. Is he on the verge of solving my sixteen-year-long medical mystery?

I continue reading: " COX was . . . about 20% of normal . . . I tend to believe that something is wrong with COX (and, maybe, other enzymes of the respiratory chain, but we did not have enough tissue to measure them)."

This is incredible! Only weeks before, he received a tiny piece of my muscle tissue that had been saved from a needle biopsy performed six years ago. From that miniscule sample he has determined that the COX enzyme, which is key in the production of energy in the body, is significantly decreased in my muscle tissue—approximately 20 percent of normal. I try to absorb the ramifications of this finding while I continue reading: "Based on the results of these studies, we may have to consider a second muscle biopsy, although we have isolated DNA from your muscle and we can start screening for mutations in some 'suspicious genes.'"

Unbelievable! Well, if they can harvest DNA from a two-thousand-year-old mummy, I guess it can't be too difficult to isolate my DNA, even if I sometimes feel worse than a mummy! My heart races as my mind swirls with reawakened possibilities for my future. If researchers can isolate a particular defect in my genes, how long will it be before they find a way to do gene therapy? Mitochondrial disease is one of the forty neuromuscular diseases being diligently researched by the Muscular Dystrophy Association. For the first time in sixteen years, I allow myself to think the unthinkable—I may eventually be cured.

After calling family and a few close friends to inform them of these significant findings, I fall into bed from exhaustion. I am in pain from my hair to my toes. But I smile as I imagine the life I once had . . . and may actually have once more.

And yet, my life can never really be the same. Even before this momentous news, my life had changed irrevocably for the better when I finally found reconciliation with the Lord.

"Thank you, Lord," I pray to the loving God, who must be rejoicing with me. "Thank you for giving me the strength to persevere long enough to see this day. And thank you for whatever you have done to bring this about. Please bless all the loving people in my life who have continually prayed for me and lifted me up throughout the years."

My eyes fill with tears. If only my mother could hear this news. She suffered with me through the early years of this horrible illness and went to her grave not knowing what struck me down in the prime of my life. What heartbreak she must have felt. Yet she never complained. She just showered me with love. I drift further and further into sleep, imagining her caring eyes and feeling the warmth of her being. What I wouldn't do for just one more hug from her . . .

"So, just ask."

"What do you mean, 'just ask'?"

"You want a hug, right? So all you have to do is ask. You deserve a hug, especially after receiving such news. You have been so persevering in searching for an answer. You never gave up, no matter how hard it was to keep going."

"I can't ask you for a hug, Mom. You are out of body."

"So are you."

"Not really, Mom. I'm just dreaming. You're dead. There's a difference."

"So let me give you a hug, and you tell me if it feels real." Her arms cradle me tightly in a loving embrace. Her touch brings tears to my eyes.

"I hope your tears don't mean that I am squeezing you too hard. It's been such a long time, and I may be a little out of practice."

"Of course not, Mom. It's just that it is so over-whelming to feel the warmth of your hug. I am crying tears of joy. But also of sorrow, because I know I am going to have to let you go."

"Go where? I told you before that I am always with you."

"It doesn't feel that way, Mom. I always seem to experience the grief of losing you more than the joy of your presence."

"You only have to believe, Beverly, and I will be there."

"That's the same thing the rabbi says about himself. Yet I find it so hard to do that sometimes."

"If you can't always feel my presence, maybe you could rely on him for support. Can't you call him anytime you want? He is a close friend of yours, isn't he?"

"I can always call upon him. But it's strange. When things are at their worst and I need him the most, I often find it the hardest to ask him for help."

"I am sure he would like to support you, particularly at those times. So why don't you pick up the phone and let him know how you are feeling?"

"Well, it's not really like that. What I have been trying to tell you is that the rabbi is not exactly a normal person."

"We all have our idiosyncrasies, Beverly. Don't let that get in the way of such a good friendship."

"It's not like that, Mom. He doesn't have any quirks. In fact, he is perfect."

"That's quite a statement, Beverly. But nobody is perfect. You, of all people, should know that, especially being a clinical psychologist."

"What I am trying to tell you is that he is perfect. And he is the most compassionate, selfless, and giving of all beings. He serves as an example to all."

"If that is what you choose to believe, I can't stop you. But remember, even the most well-intentioned person is destined to let you down sometimes. It is dangerous to idealize someone."

"Not if you idealize the ideal. He can never let me down. It is not in his nature."

"He sounds very good-hearted, Beverly. That is the most important thing in life. I am very happy that you know someone who is so giving."

"It is from you that I first learned the meaning of giving, Mom. And that's why I have been drawn to the rabbi. He stands for righteousness and preaches love for

God and one another. You first taught me these moral precepts, often by your loving example. In fact, that is your greatest legacy."

"I'm glad you feel that way, Beverly. Now, getting back to the rabbi, what's his name? You never did tell me. This good and perfect rabbi of yours must have a name."

"He does, Mom. Actually, people use many names when referring to the rabbi. Ultimately, you could say that he claims the name above all names."

"He what? What did you say?"

"Well, I didn't want to tell you this . . . I mean, I knew how much it would upset you . . . especially in your condition, with your heart and all . . . Tell me something, Mom. If dead people can hug, can they also have heart attacks? I could never go through that again . . . the numbers on the monitors sinking downward . . . the alarm when you stopped breathing . . ."

Bzzzzzzz. I awaken in a panic. The alarm clock wails . . . *she's dying . . . she's dying . . . again.*

11

IS EVERYTHING
Relative?

Circle. Circle. Circle. The chalk figures are drawn equidistant from each other on the large blackboard. The animated, neatly dressed philosophy professor pauses and points, tapping the chalkboard for emphasis. "If you are standing in this circle, you have one kind of truth. In that circle, another kind of truth. And so on, and so forth. Ultimately, truth is relative."

I stop taking notes to ponder the meaning of this statement. Meanwhile, scores of fellow students are frantically drawing geometric figures on their notepads, oblivious to these metaphysical questions. They know one absolute truth. This material will be on the next exam, and they had better capture it before the dreaded eraser demolishes the truth forever.

As the bell rings, I gather my books—along with my courage—and approach the professor. I am hooked on philosophy.

"What can I do for you?" she inquires warmly, her face still flushed with excitement at having just bestowed such monumental truths upon our impressionable young collegiate minds.

I take a deep breath and reply, "Well, I wonder if it might be possible for me to do an independent study with you next semester. I'm really interested in philosophy, and think I would benefit from a tutorial."

Her face brightens. "We should be able to arrange something," she says with an encouraging smile. "Do you have a subject in mind?"

"Existentialism," I blurt out proudly, glad that I had prepared an answer.

"Oh, that's interesting," she replies. "Do you know much about it?"

"I know a little, but I'd really like to learn more."

She nods in approval. "Okay. I'll see what I can arrange with the registrar for next semester. Why don't we talk more about it after class on Friday?"

Greatly relieved, I thank her and quickly exit the classroom. "Wow, this is going to be great," I whisper to myself. "And besides, that's one less class I'll have to compete for at registration!"

This is a major consideration. There are thousands of students at the City University of New York at Queens College, and all of them invariably end up in front of me in line at registration. I always dread the beginning of the semester, when I have to face the Queens College equivalent of a day at the track. The huge registration room fills to capacity with would-be enrollees who compete with each other for the limited number of slots set aside for each course. The walls are plastered with lists of available classes. Computer operators enter each student's selections. The challenge is to fill out the course card with a proposed class schedule as quickly as possible and race to the computer to be entered on the course rosters before each class reaches its enrollment limit.

Lines and lines of anxious, sweating students queue up in front of the row of computers. Eyes darting from one posted list to another, they hope against hope that their courses will remain open until they make it to the front of the line. Meanwhile, "human erasers" stand ready to expunge one course option after another on the large posters as the classes fill to capacity.

Given such high stakes, registration has evolved into a course in religion. For it is where the most praying takes place. I often offer a silent prayer before stepping up to the computer operator after an interminable wait and, with fingers crossed and eyes aimed skyward, hand her my punch card. The computer noisily prints out a piece of paper that contains my fate for the next semester. The operator announces, almost with sadistic glee, "Psych 201—closed . . . Psych 202—closed . . . Psych 205—closed." The long litany of rejections continues. I jump in. "What about Psych 210?" I ask nervously. "Closed." "Psych 211?" I plead, as if my life depends upon it. "Closed," the gruff voice spits back with increasing annoyance. I have overstayed my welcome, managing to actually sneak in these verbal requests illegally. The rules state that you must take your piece of paper and return to the tables to fill out yet another punch card.

After hours of braving long lines, irritable operators, and stifling heat, my fate for the next semester is finally sealed. Usually, the good news is that I have managed to enroll in courses that do not take place too early or too late in the day. There is no worse fate for a commuting student than having to brave the congested urban highways during rush hour or the dangerous streets after dark. Often, the bad news is that I have enrolled in several courses that fit my time slots but do not particularly thrill me, such as History: Since the Beginning of Time.

Who cares what happened during the Dark Ages? Actually, I do, if it takes place on Tuesdays and Thursdays between 1:30 and 3:00 P.M.

Besides registration, my other major prayer sessions occur while patrolling for a parking space in close proximity to this bustling city campus. It is a daunting task. A keen eye is needed to scout out those parked cars that are about to vacate their spaces. It is more of an art than a science. You must time a slowdown just right, allowing the requisite number of seconds necessary to assess the likelihood of a driver's imminent departure from his space.

Meanwhile, the "rocket scientist" driving the car behind you, pressing the pedal to the metal with his nose on your bumper, is scrutinizing your every move, just waiting for the opportunity to honk and yell obscenities if he detects even the slightest reduction of speed. He takes great pleasure in communicating his feelings in the most colorful, graphic displays and descriptions. This is, after all, New York City traffic. And in this chaotic labyrinth, consideration and civility have not been invented yet. Hence, prayer is always in order. Only a higher power could arrange for a prime parking space to open at just the right time, allowing you to seize the spot before being unceremoniously lambasted by the idiot behind you.

Luckily, no such parking problems will plague my commute to my philosophy tutorial. I will meet with my professor at her house, a modest, two-family walk-up in a residential section of Queens, just twenty minutes from campus. This is a blessing, not only because of the multitude of open parking spaces that line her block, but also because it provides a far more intimate, personal environment than an on-campus meeting. I am so tired of the cold, chaotic atmosphere of a large city university where a student often feels more like a pinball in a giant machine

116

than a person. This tutorial will be a unique opportunity for an in-depth, personal encounter on an intellectual level with a respected professor who will treat me like a mature adult. What an exciting prospect . . . yet unnerving, as well.

The long-awaited day of my first philosophy tutorial session has finally arrived. I nervously finger the crumpled piece of paper containing the directions as I pull into a parking space in front of my professor's house. I sigh with relief. Thankfully, I have found my way through the maze of city streets and will not be late for the first session of my independent study. I climb the stairs, take a deep breath, and ring the bell.

"Just a minute," she shouts.

I hear her footsteps approaching the door. Locks click open, and she appears, smiling.

"Come in, Beverly," she says in a warm, welcoming tone.

"Thank you," I reply, making a mental note to be even more polite than usual. I eagerly follow her up the steps to the second floor.

"Would you like a cup of coffee?"

This question is so shocking that I can hardly maintain my composure. As a lowly undergraduate, I am not used to such royal treatment.

"No, thanks, Ms.—"

"No need for such formalities here," she interrupts. "You may call me Jan."

I nod. A professor offering me a cup of coffee and her first name. This must be how Alice felt during her upside-down adventures in Wonderland.

Jan escorts me to the dining room table, where several books have been set aside for our work together. "These are the readings I thought we would use for our course," she says, apparently seeking my approval.

I glance at the esoteric titles. "Okay," I reply, already wishing I had brought along a few extra IQ points.

"Now, here is the schedule of assignments," she continues, as my mind begins to blur under the weight of the task ahead. "And, in lieu of exams, there will be a final paper."

"Fine," I say, trying to conceal my glee. My mind suddenly clears as it begins to process this unexpected bonus . . . No midterm exam. No final exam. Only a paper and a parking spot. This must be sophomore heaven.

We sit across from each other at the dining room table. Without pomp and circumstance, the course begins. Jan places an object equidistant from our relative positions and says, "Now, when you look at this object, what do you see?"

I hesitate, wondering what page this is on.

"Describe what you see," she says warmly, trying to set me at ease. It doesn't work.

"Uh . . . it's blue and white . . ."

She nods.

So far so good. At least my anxiety hasn't led to color blindness.

"What else?" she inquires.

"It has a handle on each side."

She nods again.

I force a faint smile. I am gaining confidence as we go along. Forging ahead, I do my best to describe the sugar bowl she has placed before me.

"Okay, good," she concludes. "Now I'll describe it. It has one handle . . ."

Oh no! I had said that it has two handles. This is like watching my exam being graded . . . and I've already gotten the first answer wrong.

"Why don't our descriptions match?" Jan asks.

I mull over a possible response: *Because you are the professor and you have the answer key? No . . . Because I was never really cut out for philosophy? No . . . Because I should have stayed on campus with the other drones and never exposed my inadequate brain to such lofty metaphysical questions?. . . Maybe.* Having already gotten used to the fact that I've lost my A for the course anyway, I blurt out, "Because you were describing it from where you sit, and I from where I sit?"

"Exactly!" she says with enthusiasm.

I can't believe I actually got the answer right.

Jan continues, "You described the sugar bowl from your perspective, and I from mine. Existentialists believe that each of us has his or her own experience of reality. There is no one, absolute reality. Everything is relative. There are no predetermined universal forms. Reality is comprised of the particular experiences each person has of the universe. Essence does not precede existence. Existence precedes essence.

"Let me clarify this for you. Traditionally, Western science has been essentialist in character, attempting to explain and interpret the real phenomena of the world by formulating universal abstract laws and principles that were set above and beyond any one individual being. Existential philosophy arose in opposition to this. It asserts that one's existence precedes and determines one's essence. Throughout one's lifetime, the choices a person makes in fulfilling his or her potential actually create that individual's unique essence. The method used to

119

determine one's reality is called phenomenology, an examination of the particulars of each person's experience."

I stare at her, trying to comprehend. No absolute reality . . . only my own particular experience of reality . . . no meaning outside of the meaning I give to my experience. What does this say about life? If life is defined by the meaning I ascribe to my own experiences and there is nothing beyond this to provide a context of truth, just how meaningful is life? My day-to-day experiences are certainly far from profound. If there is no way to transcend the mundane moments of life, doesn't life become meaningless? If truth is relative, is it also inconsequential? And what about God? I thought he was the ultimate, absolute truth. Where does he fit in? If God is relative, and we create him to be what we want him to be, then is he really God or just another part of our own experience?

All afternoon, we tackle these perplexing questions by examining how existentialists have attempted to solve them. We will continue to wrestle with these thorny problems as the semester progresses.

I leave the session with a wonderful feeling of excitement and adventure. I can't wait to discover how greater minds than mine have grappled with these core issues of life. I sense, however, judging from today's discussion, that I will complete this course with far more questions than answers.

As the sun begins its descent in the western sky, I head eastward back home to the suburbs. I welcome the long drive. The solitude allows me the opportunity to mull over the exciting events of the day. It is almost dark, and I arrive home far later than expected. During our philosophical musings of the afternoon, as we attempted to discover the true nature of reality, we lost track of time. I wonder how angry my mother will be. Will she be very inconvenienced by my arrival after dinner has ended? Yet, despite the late hour, I am so pleased to have spent the extra time engaged in such stimulating discussion.

I arrive in the driveway, grab my books, and run to the house.

My mother greets me with a flushed face. I am unable to determine whether it is from the heat of anger or the warmth of the kitchen. "It's so late," she comments, more out of concern than annoyance. "What happened?"

"My first philosophy tutorial session ran longer than expected," I reply, trying to reassure her that my delay was not due to some terrible mishap that will land me on the eleven o'clock news.

She looks relieved. "You must be so hungry after such a long day with work at the hospital and classes in the afternoon. That's really terrible." She showers me with enormous sympathy.

"It's not so terrible, Mom. Really. I enjoyed it." Smiling, I try out my new philosophical truth on my unsuspecting mother. "I guess it depends upon how you look at it . . . Everything is relative, you know."

12

FROM HARVARD
to Humility

August 30, 1982

"Excuse me," I say politely as I try to summon the attention of the well-dressed young man walking a few paces ahead of me. "Excuse me," I say again, smiling. Here you can't be too polite . . . or too charming. "Would you please tell me where the administration building is?"

He turns around and beams, apparently pleased that he knows the answer. "It's over there—that light-colored brick building," he says with enthusiasm, pointing to an impressive edifice. "Are you here for orientation?" he inquires, surmising from my unfamiliarity with this central structure of the hospital that I am a newcomer. They really are smart here.

"Yes. I'm a new psychology intern."

"I am, also," he offers gleefully.

I eye him for a moment. So this is one of the few good men who has been selected—along with the few good women—from hundreds of outstanding applicants, after a multitude of grueling interviews, to grace the halls of this Harvard-affiliated psychiatric hospital. He looks the part—tweed jacket, vest, briefcase, and facial hair, which must have been sprouted over the summer to enhance the effect. He has accomplished his mission. He looks exactly like Freud—that is, without the cigar. He must be saving that final touch for later this evening, when he will whip out an impressively large stogie from inside his jacket and light up in front of his jealous peers.

"I'm also headed for the administration building," he volunteers as he continues walking.

I traipse behind him, keeping track of his movements while soaking in the ambience of this revered campus. This is the jewel of the Harvard-affiliated psychiatric hospitals and the Emerald City of the world of psychology. It feels as if I have been waiting my whole life for this moment. Every blade of grass seems holy, every building part of a kingdom of exclusive wisdom. I have made it to the hallowed halls of Harvard, having studied the "religion" known as psychology for years. Now I am about to meet the gods.

I am acutely aware that this opportunity to join the Ivy League elite has not come easily. Generations of my ancestors have struggled and sacrificed to give me a chance at a better life. They were deprived of a golden invitation such as this, not only because of their poverty, but also because they were not welcome in the exclusive Ivy League. This is an entrée that I do not take lightly. It is an awesome privilege . . . but a daunting responsibility. I hope I will not fail them.

"Are you one of the psychoanalytic interns?" my walking partner inquires, attempting to make meaningful conversation.

"No, I'll be on the behavioral unit."

"Oh." His tone is a mixture of sympathy and condescension.

Psychoanalysts consider themselves to be the crème de la crème of psychology. Ever since Freud discovered the ego, his followers have made a point of enlarging theirs at every turn.

"I come from an analytic background," I quickly add, hoping to redeem myself with this credential.

"Uh-huh," he replies nonchalantly.

Since I am not a member of his exclusive club, he prefers not to invest any additional energy in me.

As we arrive at the administration building, we encounter a gathering of well-groomed, fresh-faced young adults. This must be the rest of the fortunate few, I surmise. It doesn't take an Einstein to figure this out. Almost all of the male psychoanalytic interns have apparently undergone the same transformation as my new acquaintance. It is a convention of Freudian clones. I have to laugh. To these zealous followers, Freud is the supreme god. And the greatest of all achievements is to become a living embodiment of the master himself. How is it that such well-trained psychologists, who preach the virtues of autonomy and authentic identity, so readily surrender theirs? So much for an insight-oriented approach!

Many of my colleagues are equally as enamored with Harvard as with Freud. Their very identities rest upon their Harvard affiliation. Overnight, all of us will be transformed into celebrities in the world of psychology. This exclusivity will encapsulate us in a closed world where ideas are enshrined. I am acutely aware that I must be mindful of these influences lest they narrow my perspective, possibly compromising patient care.

I have accepted this postdoctoral internship in search of knowledge more than status. Ever since I volunteered at a local psychiatric hospital during the summer of my sophomore year and was unexpectedly offered a paid position in the activities therapy department, I have realized the value of clinical experience in preparation for the practice of psychology. During graduate school, I took a position as a team leader at a private psychiatric hospital in Miami to supplement my studies . . . and my income. Experiences such as these proved invaluable in gaining insight into my chosen field. When I received my doctorate at the end of my predoctoral internship, I had the choice of taking a well-paid position or pursuing further training. I elected an additional year of training in behavioral techniques at this Harvard-affiliated teaching hospital to supplement my psychoanalytic background. I am highly committed to becoming as competent a psychologist as possible.

You could say that Dr. Joyce Brothers, the famous media psychologist, is responsible for my career choice. Well . . . at least, indirectly. The family legacy actually began in the basement, where my mother would retreat to do the laundry and iron the clothes. During these rare moments of solitude, she would religiously and reverently listen to the *Dr. Joyce Brothers Show* on the radio. My mother became so fascinated by the field of psychology that she increasingly treated my brother and me to doses of "clinical interventions" that usually began, "According to Dr. Joyce Brothers. . . ." Of course, this was expertly blended with a generous dose of Yiddish sayings combined with her unique philosophy of life. My mother was convinced that, had she been given the opportunity, she would have become a psychologist.

Because we grew up in a veritable psychologist's "office"—my mother's—it was predictable that my brother and I would gravitate toward the field of psychology. I became a clinical psychologist, and my brother a school psychologist. You might say that if my mother hadn't listened to Dr. Joyce Brothers on the radio while ironing shirts, my fate could have been very different. In fact, if permanent press had been invented at the time, I might have become a plumber.

As I make my way through the crowd, I converse with peers and supervisors alike. A sense of excitement and tension fills the air. We all know that the stakes are high. We are summoned into the administration building and led into a room that resembles an old parlor in an elite mansion. We seat ourselves around a large, polished mahogany table. Elaborately carved molding, plush carpets, and upholstered chairs uphold the Harvard image. It is somewhat intimidating. One almost feels compelled to speak in whispers for fear that the very force of one's breath might damage the facade.

We are given orientation booklets and our schedule for the week. As the meeting ends, hands are busy stuffing materials into brand-new leather briefcases, which barely give way under the assault. It will take months before these cases learn to yield to the pressure and accept more than they are designed to carry without resistance.

A small-framed woman with tortoiseshell glasses approaches me. She introduces herself as one of my supervisors. I extend a warm hello. She seems eager to converse.

After a few minutes of amenities, her expression turns deadly serious as she inquires, "Is that polyester?"

I look around, attempting to locate the reference point to her question. "What?" I ask, failing to decipher the meaning of her inquiry.

"Is that *polyester?*" she repeats, pointing to my tan jacket.

I look down, perplexed. "Um . . . maybe," I say. "I've never thought about it. It looks like some kind of gabardine, I think."

With an expression of intense disapproval, she extends her hand to touch the dreaded fabric. Her arm immediately recoils, as if she were fearful that lingering contact would undoubtedly result in hives . . . or leprosy. "You know, you shouldn't wear polyester . . . not here," she chastises.

She means at Harvard, I presume. I look at her with a puzzled expression while becoming increasingly embarrassed.

"What's wrong with polyester?" I ask naively, daring to speak that forbidden word again. I can't understand what the problem is. After all, I have just arrived from Florida, where polyester is the state fabric.

"It's just that it is not worn here. Don't you have cotton or linen clothing?"

I pause for a moment, trying to absorb the meaning of this encounter. I do not know how to reply. For months now, I have been preparing myself to answer the most difficult theoretical questions. After all, I was headed to Harvard, where I would have to match wits with the best and the brightest. But it had never occurred to me to analyze the fiber content of my wardrobe. As I fumble for a polite response I am interrupted by an admonition.

"If you don't have cotton, linen, or woolen clothing, you really must buy some."

I nod, feeling like a sorority sister who has left her sweater at home. I wonder when my skin will be allowed to touch polyester again. Probably not until I have left the Harvard system to become a civilian . . . when I cannot be reprimanded for being out of uniform.

Despite the poor reception my wardrobe has received at this exclusive private psychiatric hospital, my "shameful" polyester blazer is considered formalwear at the neighboring state hospital, where I now venture to complete my responsibilities for the day. I have no idea what to expect as I leave the driveway. This part of my internship has remained a mystery to me. My future supervisor chose not to introduce me to the grounds of the state hospital during the interview process, preferring instead to entice me with the glamour of the plush private psychiatric hospital where I have just spent my morning. It would have been poor public relations to expose me to the seedier side of the year's commitment. Better to wait for the first day of orientation, when the excitement at being part of the Harvard mystique might cushion the blow. And, if that weren't enough to prevent a sudden change of heart, then the knowledge that I had just uprooted myself from life as I knew it to fly to Boston and rent practically the last available apartment in a city with a 1 percent vacancy rate would probably do it.

I arrive at the gates of the state hospital to find a surprisingly large expanse of well-manicured lawns and meticulously trimmed bushes. Large, red-brick buildings are set apart from each other in a seemingly idyllic setting. "This is really nice," I say to myself with relief.

Spoken too soon. As I enter the door, the rank odor and the sight of the bedraggled inhabitants fill me with a sense of dread. I wonder if I should just turn around and hop on the next plane home. I decide to rehearse my resignation letter silently to myself: *I regret to inform you that I am resigning my position as a psychology intern after less than one day. I have decided to return home to Florida to become an ordinary, run-of-the-mill, polyester-clad psychologist in a nice office with a potted palm . . .*

My rehearsal is interrupted abruptly by Joan, the supervisor who had interviewed me last January. She welcomes me enthusiastically, seeming not to notice my less-than-thrilled expression. Nor does she appear to take note of the devastation and suffering that surround her. She smiles and acknowledges each patient as she navigates over and around the ones lounging on the floor, as if she were Miss Manners prancing through the ruins of the blitzkrieg, graciously serving tea. I follow her, trying to maintain my composure and not reveal the apprehension I feel.

Entering my assigned unit, my heart sinks even further. These patients appear to be even sicker and more dysfunctional than the ones I encountered in the lobby. They are the inmates who are not yet capable of being released on pass from this locked ward. As I scrutinize the eyes that beam back vacant stares, I wonder if any of these lost souls will ever be ready for even momentary freedom from this prison.

I try to smile as my remarkably caring supervisor begins introducing me to the toothless, drooling, hallucinating, babbling, snorting fellow creatures that are my new patients. Her tone is so courteous and polished that she could just as well be at a cocktail party saying, "And may I introduce to you my very close friend, the Duchess of Windsor . . ." Meanwhile, the recipients of these well-mannered introductions are on the floor, coughing, hacking, and scratching in unmentionable places.

"Hello," I say, with as much enthusiasm as I can muster. I try to find a ray of hope. I tell myself it's not so bad. Half a day down . . . a little less than a year to go.

Joan beckons me to follow her to a small room off the main corridor. She places a key in the door and ushers me into what appears to be an office. It is narrow, with shoddy desks and sagging shelves crammed against the walls. There is a barred window with an old, rusty radiator beneath it. It is a warm, late-summer day, and the air in this tiny, dusty office is oppressive. A small section of the window is propped open a few inches, providing no relief.

I am invited to take a seat, and reluctantly select one of the filthy chairs. I wish my polyester-policing supervisor could see me now— fashionably overdressed for the occasion. Joan hands me a book and begins to explain the basics of the social learning program that is being instituted on the unit as a form of token economy. It is designed to increase appropriate behaviors through reinforcement in the form of tokens, which are exchanged for tangible rewards. The goal is to shape enough appropriate behaviors so that even these severely ill, institutionalized patients can eventually be released to a less-restrictive environment. It is a monumental task.

These wounded warriors in the battle for sanity who pace these halls have fallen victim to countless failed attempts at chemical and psychotherapeutic interventions. Despite the regimens of heavy antipsychotic medication prescribed for many of these patients, the benefits have barely outweighed the costs. For the drugs often have severe, sometimes permanent, side effects that may worsen rather than resolve when the medication is withdrawn.

These patients, who have been labeled psychiatric failures by society, have been shelved into giant warehouses of human suffering, destined to be cared for by state employees who are also doing time. The government caretakers who patrol this ward are convinced that there is no hope for their pitiful charges. They have resigned themselves to a reality that we Harvard appointees refuse to acknowledge. I am warned that the state staff will do little to help and may even sabotage well-intentioned efforts to build programs that might make a difference. I wonder if these employees may actually fear such progress. After all, they are lifers who are putting in time to reap the rewards of retirement.

At the conclusion of the meeting, Joan hands me the keys to the kingdom and accompanies me to the door. I place the key in the keyhole and twist hard. The door pops open with a loud click, and we are released into the stairway. After warm good-byes, I race down the steps and leap out the door to freedom.

The fresh air rejuvenates my dulled senses. I gratefully slide into the seat of my car and make my getaway. Yet the more miles I travel, the more entrenched the scenes from the day become. I am left with perplexing and troubling questions. I have come to Harvard hoping that the truths of psychology will be revealed by the very gods themselves. I now wonder, having met the wizards of Emerald City, whether they are simply little men and women pushing levers behind a curtain, striving desperately to maintain the image of the great and powerful. Will their enshrined ideas that form the very basis of psychology be sufficient to combat such overwhelming human suffering?

I reflect upon my training and the many supervisors who have scrupulously avoided discussion of religious issues, and I wonder why. In the midst of such misery and devastation, shouldn't we contemplate the existence of a true God, a divine deity who can comfort and give hope to the hopeless, and light the darkest of nights? What's more, wouldn't even the most well-balanced individual seek solace when confronted with the harsh realities of life that inevitably spawn gnawing existential questions? Finally, in angst, mustn't we all search beyond ourselves—and psychology—for an answer to the ultimate question: "Is there a power in the universe greater than ourselves?"

13

Isn't There Someplace
Better Than This?

January 30, 1987

Beep. Beep. Beep. The relentless chirping of the persistent pager disrupts my sleep. I stir and awaken to my duty. Fumbling with the beeper on the night table, I flick off the switch. Blessed silence.

Ever since I came to Boston to complete my training nearly five years ago, I have been unable to get a full night's sleep. To make matters worse, my current position as an associate director of a regional nursing-home program requires that I be on twenty-four-hour call.

Reaching for the light, I prop myself up on the pillow, grab the phone, and proceed to dial.

"Hello. Geriatric Services . . ." The cheery voice on the other end reminds me that some people are actually awake at 3 A.M. and may even enjoy it.

"Hello, this is Dr. Rose. You paged me?"

"Yes, Dr. Rose," the perky voice acknowledges, sounding as if it were the middle of the day rather than the dead of night. "Peaceful Rest Nursing Home has left an urgent message that you call them right away. The number is—"

"That's okay," I interrupt. The shorter the conversation at this hour the better. "I have the number, thank you." I stare across the room and spot my briefcase lying on the floor next to the dresser. It contains my telephone directory. But the thought of braving the cold, hardwood floors so early on a frigid winter morning to retrieve a phone number prompts me to reconsider. "Wait a minute," I request. "Would you please give me the number?" Memorizing the digits, I hang up the phone and dial.

"Hello. Peaceful Rest Nursing Home . . ."

"Hello, this is Dr. Rose. I received an urgent message to call you."

"Oh yes, Dr. Rose. Please hold."

The reception is far too friendly. They must need help badly. This is not a good sign.

"Dr. Rose?"

"Yes."

"Hold on a second. I'll transfer you to the nurse in charge."

Usually my contacts are met with mild indifference unless there is a crisis. A psychologist providing services to a nursing home consults with staff about patients who, for one reason or another, can't quite hack it in the system. Nursing homes are regimented settings where the entire routine can be disrupted by one unruly patient. We are the gramps-busters. Who else ya gonna call?

"Dr. Rose?" A less-than-elated voice comes on the line. "Mr. Jones has torn off all his clothes and is running naked in the yard."

I feel like blurting out, "So why are you calling me? Put a coat on the poor gentleman and escort him inside." That, however, would be unprofessional. A psychologist is supposed to be patient, understanding, and compassionate in all circumstances, even when aroused from a deep sleep on a freezing cold New England morning at 3 A.M. Trying to stifle my annoyance, I ask politely, "What have you done to try to retrieve him?"

She replies, "We tried to catch him."

"And what happened?" I ask.

"He escaped and kept running around the yard."

I wonder how a staff of nurses and aides half his age cannot catch a naked eighty-eight-year-old grandfather. Maybe he snatched the Preparation H from the nurses' station and oiled his body like a wrestler in order to elude their grasp before making his great escape. The picture in my mind is just too much to imagine at 3 A.M., even for a seasoned psychologist.

"Well," I say, with as much authority as possible, "if you are unable to handle him, you will have to have him transported to the inpatient unit at the hospital."

The line goes dead as the nurse pauses for an interminable length of time. I fully expect her to ask that I come down there in the middle of the night with a butterfly net to bag him for her.

Finally, she speaks. "Well," she says hesitantly, "okay, if you think that's best . . ."

"I do," I reply, sounding more adamant. "It's unfortunate, but if he can't be contained in the home, this is the only option to preserve his safety. I assume he has been taking his meds?"

"Oh yes. Of course!" she retorts sharply as if I've asked a stupid question. "We always make sure he takes his meds."

Any insinuation to the contrary, however well-intentioned, invariably produces an indignant response. Nevertheless, I am always brave enough to ask.

"Then this would be a good opportunity to have him thoroughly reevaluated physically and psychologically to determine the cause of the problem."

She isn't pleased with my answer but offers no retort, "Okay, Dr. Rose," she says half-heartedly. "Thank you." *For nothing,* she probably wants to add but restrains herself.

"You're welcome," I say, trying to sound upbeat.

As I fall back on the pillow, I picture good old Mr. Jones, in the buff, jumping over bushes, sliding into snowbanks, and driving every member of the staff crazy. It just may be his last hurrah, his chance to go out on a high note. I smile, roll over, and try to get some sleep.

Beep. Beep. Beep. I am abruptly awakened for a second time. It is now 7 A.M. It's wishful thinking to hope for a full night's sleep when you are responsible for supervising twenty psychologists and therapists who consult to forty nursing homes. Although, it would take more than sleep to rejuvenate this sick, tired body that has been fighting a progressively disabling illness for more than three years now.

I dial the service again. I am informed that this time the message is from my office. I call in and am told to report at 10 A.M. for an administrative meeting—something about bureaucratic issues and reorganization. I am not pleased. I had planned to spend my time this morning at a nursing home. Once again, the important matters of patient care must take a backseat to administrative concerns.

I arrive promptly for the meeting and sit there half asleep. The session drones on and on until everyone is totally bored. One of the few benefits of being an associate director is that I can utilize my influence to end a meeting. So I soon suggest we adjourn. I receive the first enthusiastic response of the day from my lethargic colleagues. I head out the door for my nearest nursing home.

Parking my car, I grab my briefcase and walk toward the front entrance. I try to ignore the increasing fatigue and achiness that are slowing me down earlier and earlier each day. The wheelchair brigade is lined up in the front lobby like a receiving line at a bar mitzvah. The thin, frail, feeble occupants can barely acknowledge my presence. They sit propped up like floppy rag dolls with flaccid limbs that remain in fixed, unnatural positions for hours at a time. I smile and say hello to each resident while feeling assaulted by the sights and smells that smack me in the face with every visit. While my nose eventually habituates to the odors, my eyes cannot adapt to the sight of lonely, sick, suffering elderly residents who will probably live out the remainder of their lives in this awful place.

What can I bring to them to make their plight more tolerable? What great rescue can I perform? I call on everything I have ever learned and experienced to try to understand and make a difference. There are some therapeutic triumphs, often due to medication changes or even psychotherapy. But the failures far outweigh the successes. These frail elderly residents present complicated cases. They have a multitude of medical problems necessitating multiple medications, each with side effects. In addition, many suffer from an array of psychological problems. It is difficult to determine exactly what is causing what.

In the fields of psychology and neuropsychology, diagnostic tools are far from perfect, and reaching a definitive diagnosis can be extremely difficult. A psychologist can become intrigued by the challenge, interested in the complexities, and enamored with the science. But ultimately, in working with the institutionalized elderly, one must come to terms with the intense suffering of lonely, fragile senior citizens who are spending their last days in undignified, unfamiliar, and harsh surroundings, deprived of the love and caring they so desperately need and deserve. For those of us in the helping professions who care so deeply about people, this heartbreaking scenario is sometimes too much to bear.

When I return home, I immediately head for the shower to cleanse my body of the putrid odors of the day. Cleansing my conscience will take far more than soap and water. It is a sad reality that the solutions our society has instituted to care for our oldest and wisest loved ones have frequently failed to alleviate their suffering and, oftentimes, have even intensified their misery. My mind fills with images of bedraggled bodies trapped in wheelchairs and scantily dressed, drooling, institutionalized psychiatric patients languishing in dilapidated day rooms. *Why, God? Why won't you rescue humanity from such suffering . . . and from our own shameful solutions?*

As droplets of water trickle down my face like tears, I wonder how we as psychologists can foster the healing of such shattered spirits. I hope these patients can soothe their suffering souls through summoning faith in a higher power . . . as I struggle to find faith of my own.

Fighting exhaustion, I massage my aching limbs in an attempt to reduce the pain. This provides little relief. I have been battling increasingly disabling symptoms since the second half of my postdoctoral internship three and a half years ago. I have consulted numerous specialists and tried many medications. The doctors recognize that my symptoms are uncannily similar to those that disabled both my grandmother and aunt in the prime of their lives. Yet the medical profession still does not have the technology to provide a conclusive diagnosis, especially in the area of genetic diseases.

I have reached the point of resignation. Tomorrow, at the age of thirty-four, after years of struggling to maintain my career with increasingly failing health, I will walk into my supervisor's office and relinquish my position. It will be one of the worst days of my life.

PART 3

The Answer
IS LOVE

———————⚬———————

And now these three remain:
faith, hope and love.
But the greatest of these is love.

1 CORINTHIANS 13:13

14

PLEASE DON'T WEEP
for Me

December 13, 1998

"Today is the greatest day of my life!" I exclaim. The figure in the mirror smiles back at me in approval. So far I am a hit. Let's see what happens when I deliver this speech later this morning in front of an audience that will be slightly less biased. "Why is this day so special?" I continue, adjusting my inflection to achieve the proper emphasis.

I pause to take note of the gray hair that is increasingly ravaging my fading brown locks like crabgrass infiltrating an unattended lawn. "But I am only forty-six," I appeal to the salt-and-pepper entanglement, as if pleading with the alien strands will send these unwelcome invaders scurrying to some other, older head. Oh well, my mother also grayed at too early an age. I sigh with resignation. Genetics—the amazing biological blueprint that endowed me with so many talents . . . and, apparently, the curse that short-circuited my life. Ever since I walked into my supervisor's office twelve years ago to resign, my life has been consumed by this illness. I fear my prime has passed, along with dreams of marriage, family, and career. And yet, I stand here in front of this mirror proclaiming today to be the greatest day of my life!

I reach for my toothbrush, tipping over the small memorial candle glass that has been converted into a toothbrush holder. Necessity is the mother of invention. "And mothers are a necessity," I whisper, thinking of the irreplaceable woman I miss so much. It's been eight months since this tiny glass sheltered the glowing memorial candle on the anniversary of her death . . . and eleven years of candles. I stare at the empty glass, remembering the fragile flame that flickered as my tears flowed. And yet, this year, the candle lighting ignited such reassuring images of my mother coming back in a dream to comfort me in my sorrow. Or did she come to hear the truth?

I smile, remembering my struggle, even in a dream, to break the news to her about him, "my rabbi . . . friend." *Very clever, Beverly.* If she were alive, would I have the courage to say even that much . . . let alone invite her to my speech today? Too bad Ed can't be here. He would attend if he didn't live so far away. And Dad would surely come if he were well enough to make the trip from Florida to Boston. Thankfully, at age eighty-seven, he still entertains with his ukulele and even leads a choral group that visits condominiums and nursing homes. But the long trip would be just too tiring for him. Thank God, my wonderful friends will be there. They are like family to me.

Emerging from the bathroom, I slowly make my way to the kitchen, passing by the fluffy pink blanket spread out on the floor. It will remain there for the time being, even though its canine occupant is far away. I refuse to believe that my beloved Shih Tzu, Jennifer, will not be well enough to return home from the animal hospital—not after all these prayers.

I glance at the clock. Although I've only been up for an hour, I am already exhausted from my morning routine. Nevertheless, I have a speech to give. I reach for my coat and, with notes in hand, head out the door for service.

Reaching my destination, I park my car and slowly make my way toward the long staircase leading to the colonial-style, clapboard building. Raising my weary leg, I take the first step and am lifted up—not entirely under my own power. With renewed passion, my body struggles upward step by step.

How I wish I could have had more rest before this momentous occasion. But how could I, having made trips back and forth to the animal hospital all week to visit Jennifer in the ICU? What a time for a dog to collapse and have to be rushed to the emergency room, barely alive. What am I saying? There is no good time for the companion you have loved and nurtured for thirteen years to suddenly drop from a burst tumor on the spleen and require emergency surgery. An icy wind stings my eyes, hastening tears to flow as I envision my usually bright-eyed, bushy-tailed Shih Tzu now barely clinging to life, her small, furry body shivering and panting in the ICU cage. Will I arrive this afternoon to face the unbearable decision of whether or not to put her to sleep to spare her further suffering? Might she even die before I return to visit her?

"Good morning, Beverly." A neatly dressed woman with an engaging smile greets me at the door, handing me a program.

"Good morning." I smile back.

"Beautiful day, isn't it?" she continues, with eager anticipation of more pleasantries.

"Yes," I squeak, my voice barely tested for this first encounter of the day. One of the many disadvantages of living alone is that the vocal cords warm up in public.

I am ushered to one of the few unoccupied seats. I survey my surroundings. The sanctuary is filled to capacity. Even the balcony is bulging. There must be three hundred people here, I reflect nervously as I try to muster the courage to speak in front of such a large audience. Immersed in thought, I hardly notice the beginning of the service. I wonder how long it will be before I am summoned to the podium. Suddenly I am aroused from my reveries by the mention of my name.

". . . And I've asked Beverly to come, if you would at this time, to share your story . . ." I take a deep breath and force my aching muscles from my seat.

"Beverly has a wonderful story to tell, and I thought that during this holiday season . . ."

Slowly, I make my way down the long aisle.

"We've prayed for her so regularly. She's been so sick for so many years . . . and she's coming today under tremendous distress because her dog, Jennifer, is not doing well at all. And she is going to find out today whether the dog might have cancer. Jennifer has been her companion for the last thirteen years, her devoted friend while she's been so sick."

Arriving at the stairs leading up to the platform, I will my muscles to move. They obey.

"So, Beverly, it is a privilege to welcome you here."

Climbing laboriously up the steps, I reach the pulpit winded. The expectant congregants seem to wait with bated breath. As I open my mouth to speak, the sanctuary dims to a blur, and I am miraculously embraced by a familiar, loving presence. He entered my life nearly two years ago when I was blinded by despair from long years of suffering and disability. As soon as I knew him, I loved him. Through him, I have gained new meaning in my life and a rebirth of hope and spiritual healing. In him, I have found the strength to persevere through the pain. Because of him, I stand here today and serve in his name—the name above all names. He is the Way, the Truth, the Life. He is the Gate, the Living Water, the Good Shepherd. He is the Lord!

I step forward, and as my words take wing, I publicly proclaim his name—the name of the rabbi—the precious name of Jesus Christ—for the first time in my life:

> Good morning. Today is the greatest day of my life, and I am so pleased that you are here to share it with me. Why is this day so special? Am I here to receive an award? No. Have I just won the lottery? No. Am I getting married today? No. But I'll entertain all offers after the service. The reason this is the greatest day of my life is because the Lord lifted me out of a sickbed today so that I could come before you to attest to the truth and boundless love of Jesus Christ.
>
> I have many loving friends in this congregation. Yet some of you may not know me. It would be difficult in the few moments I have this morning to fully describe my background. But if you visit any public or university library and proceed to the reference section, you will see two large red volumes entitled *Who's Who in America*. You can look me up in the latest edition. I'm listed there. You have probably heard of this prestigious list of Americans, which includes such notables as Alexander Graham Bell, Eleanor Roosevelt, Thurgood Marshall, and Bill Gates. So, you may wonder what I am doing among these famous and illustrious people.

I am a clinical psychologist who had a fair number of accomplishments in my field before falling ill more than a decade and a half ago. I had held an academic appointment at Harvard Medical School and was about to earn a six-figure income in my position as an associate director of a regional nursing-home program.

I was born into an observant Jewish family and attended temple services from an early age, particularly on the High Holy Days. By the time I was thirty, I had already achieved lofty professional goals and thought I was in line with my God. By all accounts, I thought I had it all. What I didn't know was that my life would take a radically different course that would change the very person I was . . . and would become.

For, at age thirty-one, shortly after receiving my Harvard appointment, I began to experience severe fatigue and painful, weak muscles. After almost four years of struggling to meet professional responsibilities with progressively failing health, I was forced to acknowledge the futility of the endeavor and resign my position. I was compelled to relinquish my apartment in the Boston area, which I could no longer afford, and move in with my parents in Florida. Two and a half months later, my mother died unexpectedly. By that time, I had become totally bedridden from the illness. But, please don't weep for me. For, years later, in the confines of that very sickbed where I cried and railed against God and life, *I met Jesus Christ.*

When you are stripped of all the seemingly most

important things in life—profession, prestige, money, apartment, and, especially, a loving mother—and are left in bed to suffer the ravages of a devastating illness, you scream out to the universe for answers. Deriving little comfort from faith in my own religion, I read many books on world religions and prayed to the "universal divine force" through earnest meditation. But I still received few answers . . . and little comfort. I was in agonizing despair, felt desperately alone, and believed that, given the severity of my disability, my life could no longer have any purpose or meaning. "What kind of a God would leave me here to suffer this most horrible fate?" I cried out in the midst of such devastation.

Then I took the one action that would change my life forever. I did the one thing I thought I would never do. I picked up a book and read about Jesus Christ. I learned how Jesus had implored the Jewish people to follow him, and I suddenly realized that this invitation also applied to me. Granted, two thousand years had passed. But, imagining myself standing in that crowd of Jews listening to the compelling truth of Jesus, I knew that he meant those words for *me* . . . now . . . today.

As I lay in bed, overcome by exhaustion, pain, and despair, I closed my weary eyes and, from the depths of the abyss, began to whisper the name of Jesus over and over again. Suddenly, an awesome, loving presence filled my body and soul. I knew it was *Jesus Christ himself,* coming to answer my pleas with his warm, embracing presence.

Since that fateful day almost two years ago, I have studied intensively about Jesus and Christianity through seminary courses and countless popular books. And my mind has confirmed what my heart already knew. As Philip Yancey phrases it in *Disappointment with God,* "God responded to the question of unfairness not with words, but with a visit, an Incarnation. And Jesus offers flesh-and-blood proof of how God feels about unfairness, for he took on the 'stuff' of life, the physical reality at its unfairest. He gave, in summary, a final answer to all lurking questions about the goodness of God."

In *Where Is God When It Hurts?* Yancey tells us precisely how the Son of God reacted to life's unfairness: "When he met a person in pain, he was deeply moved with compassion. . . . When Jesus' friend Lazarus died, he wept. . . . [W]hen Jesus himself faced suffering, . . . [h]e recoiled from it, asking three times if there was any other way." Because Jesus walked the earth as an embodiment of the living God, I, a Jew who has become a believer, can now know with certainty that God not only cares for me and understands my suffering . . . but even weeps for me.

Knowing Jesus has changed every moment of my life and everything I am. Now I spend my previously despairing and unproductive hours striving to emulate Christ each day through thought and action. For Jesus not only shows me living proof of who God is, but also who he wishes me to be. As T. W. Hunt so eloquently states in his book *The Mind of Christ,* God "became like us so we might become like Him. . . . He went from birth to death living our kind of life to give us an example of what God meant man to be." The apostle Paul reminds us in Colossians 3:10, to "put on the new self, which is being renewed in knowledge in the image of its Creator."

In Christ, I strive to turn my anger into love, my bitterness into compassion, and my feelings of being cheated in life into efforts to bring about bounties for others. And, unlike the many times my illness has prevented me from physically performing good deeds, I can succeed every day in the service of the Lord despite my disability. For, no matter what my circumstances, I can fulfill the Lord's greatest commandments to love him and to love others. There is no disability that can ever handicap a person who strives to faithfully serve Jesus Christ.

In *Where Is God When It Hurts?* Philip Yancey tells a true story about a man, Christian Reger, whom he met while visiting the grounds of Dachau, a Nazi concentration camp. Reger was a member of the Confessing Church, a segment of the state church in Germany, which openly took a stand against Hitler. Sadly, the church organist handed him over to the Nazis, who imprisoned him at Dachau for four years. After gaining his freedom, Reger worked with the International Dachau Committee to restore the camp as a memorial to remind humankind that such atrocities must never happen again.

Reger told Yancey of a remarkable incident that occurred shortly after his confinement and caused him to have renewed hope and belief in the presence of God. At Dachau, each inmate was permitted to receive one letter per month. A month after his arrival, Reger received correspondence from his wife. At the conclusion of her remarks, she had written a Bible reference along the bottom margin. It was Acts 4:26–29, which ends, "Now, Lord, behold their threatenings: and grant unto thy servants, that with all boldness they may speak thy word" [KJV].

That afternoon, Reger was taken to a room to await interrogation. He feared he would be pressured to reveal the identities of members of his church, who would then be arrested and, most likely, killed. Trembling, he waited outside the room. A fellow minister emerged, inconspicuously placed something into Reger's pocket, and departed. Reger had never met the man before. When Reger was taken in for questioning, he dreaded the inevitable beating for not surrendering the names of his fellow Christian believers. But, remarkably, the session was nonviolent.

After returning to the barracks, Reger remembered the encounter with the stranger. He placed his hand in his pocket and discovered a matchbox. He opened the box, believing that the minister had kindly slipped him matches, an invaluable commodity for an inmate. Instead, he discovered only a piece of paper. It contained a notation: Acts 4:26–29. Miraculously, it was an exact match to the biblical reference his wife had sent him. Reger believed that God had orchestrated this demonstration to reassure him of his presence. Reger told

Yancey, "God did not rescue me and make my suffering easier. He simply assured me that he was alive, and knew I was here."

Reger offered the following insight, which so profoundly applies to my own life: "Nietzsche said a man can undergo torture if he knows the Why of his life. . . . But here at Dachau, I learned something far greater. I learned to know the Who of my life. He was enough to sustain me then, and is enough to sustain me still."

I ask you to consider making today the greatest day of your life. For you have been blessed with the strength of body and spirit to come here to his holy house today to worship with his loving body in this beautiful sanctuary . . . in the presence of a Lord who deeply loves you, provides for you, responds to the very whisper of his name, weeps for you, will never leave you, and has reserved a place for you in heaven. Don't wait for the earthly prizes of prestige, wealth, or possessions to bring you the elusive happiness you seek. Find joy now, today, in knowing that you have all the riches one could ever hope for or desire in Jesus Christ. Consider seeking, accepting, and celebrating the presence of Jesus Christ in your life.

To the publisher of *Who's Who in America,* I make this request: Please save ink and paper, and replace the details of my long biographical entry with these four words that best summarize my greatest accomplishments—*Follower of Jesus Christ.*

There is a pause. Suddenly, a thunderous burst of applause rings out from this usually reserved congregation. The ovation seems to go on forever. I survey the smiling, tearful faces of the congregants. One by one, they rise to their feet until everyone is standing, except for . . . except for a woman in the very last pew.

> *No . . . That couldn't be . . . It's impossible . . . She looks like . . . No . . .*

I blink several times, hoping to erase the vision from my sight. The roar of the applause grows louder.

> *She can't be here. She's dead. Dead and buried. The woman glares at me with accusing eyes. I stare back in disbelief. "So that's who the rabbi is?" the woman seems to scream at me across the pews. "JESUS CHRIST? After all I taught you, you come here to a church in front of all these goyim and talk blasphemy!"*
>
> *I want to plead with my accusing mother, "But he's not who you think he is."*

Instead I stand dumbfounded, hoping that the applauding congregants will mistake my shocked expression for a look of disbelief at the incredibly long standing ovation.

As I make my way down the aisle toward the back of the church, well-wishers embrace me with warm hugs and kind words. Pastor Dave greets me enthusiastically.

"Well, I've never seen that happen before in all the years I've been here—a standing ovation!"

I smile while looking past him at the figure of the woman. She is heading out the door. Pushing my aching muscles to the limit, I catch up to her just as she is about to make her way down the steps. I grasp her shoulder from behind. She turns around with a startled expression.

"Oh!" she says, somewhat shocked by the contact. Recognizing me, she beams a smile. "Beautiful speech, Beverly. I really enjoyed it. It was so inspiring."

Embracing me warmly, she departs, leaving me to stand there . . . and wonder.

You would have liked him if you had known him, I murmur to myself as I attempt to calm my disquieted mind. She is silent.

The long, winding road stretches before me. The car groans as it heads uphill, leaving the church far behind. Yet the invading vision of my angry, accusing mother yelling from the back of the sanctuary refuses to yield. Pressing hard on the accelerator, I gather speed, hoping to somehow leave the disturbing intrusion behind. A church spire comes into view, an ironic backdrop to my charging thoughts. I recall riding with my mother one day as we passed an abandoned temple. "Remember, Beverly," she admonished, "the worst sin of all is for a temple to be converted into a church." Have I committed an even greater sin in her eyes?

A tear trickles down my cheek. My face has become accustomed to the constant wetness of weeping during the past week. With Jennifer barely clinging to life, there have been many agonizing, tearful moments. My precious dog, who has comforted me throughout the long hours of my illness for all these years, has become like a child to me. The thought of losing her is unbearable. *Yet, Mom, how much more must you be suffering as you imagine you have lost me to Jesus? You haven't. I am no less Jewish now than I was before . . . just more Christian. Can you understand that my love for Jesus completes me as a Jew?*

The miles drone on and on. It is a long trip to the veterinary hospital, and I am not eager to reach my destination. The veterinarian was far from optimistic yesterday. Jennifer may no longer be alive by the time I arrive. The highway is hypnotic, leaving my mind to drift aimlessly. The trees and bushes lining the road fade into the background as my thoughts grow louder . . .

> *"Slow down, you'll get us both killed!"*
>
> *"What?" I exclaim to the invading voice.*
>
> *"I said, 'Slow down.' You know how dangerous these roads are. You never know what the other driver will do. You have to drive defensively. Unless, of course, your Jesus will save you!"*
>
> *"Very funny, Mom. You always did have a great sense of humor."*
>
> *"Yes, Beverly, about most things. But not about this."*
>
> *"I know how upset you are, Mom, but let me explain."*
>
> *"What's there to explain? The rabbi you are so fond of is Jesus Christ, and Jesus Christ is your God. So you are a goy just like your father. No . . . even worse. At least your father didn't go off to some church and become a Christian!"*

"It's not like that. I didn't just go off somewhere to convert. I have found God."

"I didn't know he was lost!"

"Another good one, Mom. Obviously, he wasn't lost. But I was. I lay in my sickbed year after year, fervently searching for God, but I could not find him. I was convinced he had abandoned me. Then I realized that maybe I couldn't find him because I didn't know who I was looking for. After all, Jewish scholars define God in the negative—who he isn't. It is difficult to look for someone who is not. Whoever they claim he is . . . or isn't, he seemed to be a distant, impersonal, and uncaring Being who left me to suffer alone in terrible sickness, grieving my overwhelming losses.

"Then I came to know Jesus. And he revealed a personal God to me—one who cares deeply about me, is faithful and abiding in his love, and yearns for relationship with me. Now I no longer feel alone in my misery, for I know that I am not alone."

"You were lonely, Beverly, so you looked elsewhere for support. That's all . . . sick and lonely. I have always said that the worst thing that can happen to a person is to become sick, poor, and lonely."

"I may be sick and poor, Mom, but I am not that lonely. I have the Lord and wonderful friends, many of whom are part of my new family of believers."

"If only I hadn't died, Beverly. I could have sat with you and comforted you so you wouldn't have become so

distraught that you had to resort to this. What a terrible shame!"

"It is not a shame. It's something to proclaim!"

"What is so wrong with being Jewish that you had to go find Jesus to worship?"

"It's not that Judaism is wrong, Mom. I just don't think the story stops there. I believe that God wanted to show us what he is really like, so he revealed himself in Jesus, who was, you must remember, a Jew. Having met Jesus, I now know for certain who my God is."

"How can you meet God? No one can stand face to face with God."

"That's just it, Mom. We can. We can see God in Jesus. And Jesus not only stood face to face with us, but hand in hand."

"Jesus is not God, Beverly. There is only one God."

"Jesus is an embodiment of our one God, Mom."

"You can play word games if you wish. But your God is not my God."

"We have the same God, Mom. And he appeared on earth through Jesus to reconcile us to him." I fear reconciliation with my mother may take an even greater miracle.

"What do you mean 'reconcile us to him'? I don't understand why God would come into the world as a human being. Such a powerful deity doesn't have better things to do than to bother coming to earth—in the form of a man, yet?"

"That's the beauty of it, Mom. He comes in search of us because he loves us and desires to be loved in return. He will go to any length to reach out to us—even to appear incarnate and die on a cross so that we might live through him."

"What do you mean 'live through him'?"

"Through his death we know we have eternal life. And in his life, Jesus reveals what we should be. Our task is to take on the mind of Christ more and more throughout our lives."

"So he took on the image of man so that all of us could become more like God? Sounds far-fetched."

"It is, Mom. It's a miracle. And, what is so extraordinary is that, through the incarnation, God experienced what it is like to be human. So we can rest assured that he truly understands."

"An omniscient God should already know."

"I'm sure you're right. But I think he did it to reassure us that he understands our suffering because he has walked in our shoes."

"Why should it make such a difference to you now, Beverly, after all these years? The Jewish God was good enough for you before."

"He is the same God, Mom, as I already told you. And the difference was revealed to me through suffering."

"What do you mean 'through suffering'?"

"You know how often I have wrestled with metaphysical questions regarding the meaning of life and the

nature of God and man. Even as a young child, I challenged your religious beliefs and practices."

"I remember all too well. You always were precocious and had such an inquisitive mind. You take after me in that regard. I told you about the porcelain doll that broke when I dropped it trying to see what was underneath her dress. I was such a curious child, just like you . . . and I still see nothing wrong with it."

"It's really admirable that you feel that way, Mom, especially since you were punished for your curiosity by your mother, who never bought you another doll."

"Some things are more important, Beverly."

"I know, Mom. I have always respected your courage to question. You have taught me never to be afraid to ask questions. In fact, doesn't Judaism actually encourage us to question?"

"You're right, Beverly. But I hate to see you so troubled."

"I appreciate your concern, Mom. But, thank God, my quest led me to answers."

"Perhaps not the right answers, Beverly . . . at least not the ones I taught you. Maybe I just didn't do a good enough job."

"You did. You did an excellent job in raising me in an observant Conservative Jewish home. But despite my adherence to Jewish rituals and practices, I just couldn't feel the presence of a personal, caring God. And I never understood why.

"To make matters worse, as I grew older, I became

*cognizant of so much injustice and suffering in the world.
I struggled to come to terms with the pogroms that killed
much of your family, the horrible deprivation you experienced as a sick and impoverished child, the Holocaust
that claimed the lives of so many Jews and non-Jews, the
racial violence in Brooklyn, so many Israeli wars. Over
and over again, I found myself confronted by the haunting question, How could a loving and powerful God
bear witness to all that suffering and do nothing? I won-
dered whether maybe God simply doesn't exist. Or, if he
does, is he just too distant and uncaring? Since I could
not feel his presence, I struggled to think my way to the
truth. I read all sorts of books on theology and took philosophy courses to probe existential issues."*

*"I remember all those nights when you arrived
home late. You were so exhausted."*

*"I was tired but intellectually exhilarated. Yet for
some reason, I felt even more distant from God. Finally,
I turned to a different kind of truth—psychology."*

*"That may be an interesting way to study human
beings. But that is no religion, Beverly."*

*"Believe it or not, Mom, for some people it is. But not
for me. As a psychologist, I was suddenly confronted daily
with anguished souls pacing the corridors of psychiatric
hospitals and nursing homes. There was only so much I
could realistically do to help those distraught patients. No
psychological theory or technique alone could alleviate
such overwhelming suffering. I was left, once again, to*

search for an elusive, higher Being. Yet I tried hard to keep my existential angst from becoming all consuming. Somehow, at the end of the day, I was able to shelve such questions . . . that is, until tragedy struck me down."

"I had no idea it had been so difficult for you, Beverly."

"The worst was yet to come, Mom. When I was stricken with this horrible illness, the extreme suffering and extraordinary loss brought me to the very edge of existence. Almost everything I ever held dear was stripped from me. I felt cast aside, banished from the mainstream of life to confront the meaning of it all. There was no 'life clutter' to obscure my view or distort my vision. I stared straight into the abyss and struggled to see form or shape . . . I saw nothing. I screamed . . . I heard nothing.

"Lost in a spiritual wilderness, I came upon an invitation from the rabbi of Nazareth to first-century Jews to follow him. I was profoundly moved. He seemed so loving, so compelling, so true. I knew he meant his words for me.

"Lying there in my sickbed, I marshaled every ounce of strength I had left and willed my lips to whisper just one word—the Word—Jesus. That tiny gesture born of such monumental effort ushered in the most breathtaking presence I had ever experienced. It was Jesus coming to answer my plea, to fill the void, to turn the darkness to light. At that awesome moment, in the depths of despair, paralyzed by unimaginable suffering, I finally felt the loving presence of God. Jesus had come to rescue me."

"Why should the powerful, loving, and personal

God that you claim Jesus to be allow you to go through such horrendous pain, Beverly, let alone allow such suffering in this world? Just hearing what you have been through has brought tears to my eyes."

"The answer is love, Mom."

"I think all this driving is making your head spin."

"No, really, the answer is love. In love, our God gives us free will so that we can enter into an authentic, freely loving relationship with him. If we were programmed to love him, would it truly be love?"

"So how does that tie in with suffering?"

"People don't always use their free will for the good. I have come to the conclusion that much of our suffering has been brought about by humanity—or rather by our lack of humanity. Many of the anguishing questions that prompted me to seek out a higher Being to explain—and ultimately blame—for the horrors in this world can be answered in our own inhumanity toward each other:

"Who tortured and murdered thousands and thousands of innocent men, women, and children in the pogroms?

"Who was responsible for the poverty of immigrants like your parents who were forced to abandon homes and professions in Russia to save their lives, only to be reduced to selling inferior goods from a pushcart to feed their starving families in American ghettos?

"Who was ultimately responsible for your death from complications after your heart-valve replacement?

163

That surgery was necessitated by damage from rheumatic fever that you contracted when you were physically vulnerable because your parents were forced to raise you in such appalling conditions. Such poverty can be traced back to the pogroms and even filtered down to a third generation—my generation—leaving me to pace the floors every night worrying whether you and Dad would return home alive from a ghetto store that you could barely afford to rent.

"Who created all the racial tension, hatred, and violence in that Brooklyn neighborhood? And who was ultimately responsible for all the starving ghetto children playing in the filthy streets in worn-out clothes . . . children whose ancestors were slaves?

"Who was responsible for the torture and brutal murder of millions of Jews and non-Jews in the Holocaust?

"Who was responsible for all the wars throughout history that claimed so many lives?

"I'll tell you who was responsible for all these horrors—people who hate! The ultimate irony of life is that a loving God gave us free will so that we might freely love him and each other. And we have perverted this most precious of God-given gifts, using it instead to freely hate. Can you imagine the excruciating pain God must feel as he watches us ravage the beautiful world he created? It must take incredible restraint for such a powerful and loving Being not to wave his hand and miraculously clean up each and every mess

we make. Yet he stands by and patiently suffers along with us. For his love is so great that he would rather bear the grief that comes from our propensity to hate than deprive us of the freedom to love."

"Those are very inspiring thoughts, Beverly. But what about your illness?"

"I struggle with that question every day. I don't think that such a loving God would directly send my illness. Maybe it can be explained as just a part of nature, like violent storms and earthquakes. We don't live in the Garden of Eden, you know. Yet I believe the Lord hears our prayers. Why he grants some of our requests and not others we cannot know. Only God knows his plans for us.

"But what is so terribly distressing is that we ourselves have disrupted the natural design, defiling nature through our careless disregard for his creation. This has led to all kinds of human misery that we often look to God to solve. I believe that God does perform miracles. But mostly, he endows us with the ability to solve problems and find cures by giving us the intelligence and resources to do it. He hopes we will use our free will to choose to do good. Can you imagine what would happen if we opted to pool our resources to combat disease and preserve the environment instead of spending billions on wars, addictions, and frivolous pursuits? How many ailments we could have conquered by now. What a healthier, life-enhancing world we would all inhabit!"

"A lot of lofty thoughts, Beverly. But not very realistic, I'm afraid."

"And yet I am not afraid, Mom. I feel comforted regardless of not always knowing the why—because I know the Who. And that is Jesus. He is the answer to suffering because, through him, God demonstrated that he loves me, understands my suffering, weeps for me, and will be with me forever. And I believe, Mom, that while God did not send my suffering, he gives me the strength to endure my hardships and uses my suffering to bring about good. He even lifts me up from my sickbed, inspiring me to write a book that will hopefully help others to cope with the pain in their lives."

"Well, if it helps you to know that you are helping others, I'm happy for you."

"It does, Mom. But it is even more than that. Jesus came to teach us by example to love God and to love one another as he loves us. In caring for others, I am not just fulfilling a commandment. I am expressing my love for the One who loved me first. We, his followers who form the body of Christ, are a family, serving him by serving others in love. It is all about love."

"You know how much I love you, Beverly."

"I know, Mom."

"As much as any human being can love another."

"I know."

"But I can never accept Jesus as God. I am a Jew. And it goes against my very grain because of everything

I believe, not to mention the way I was brought up and all I have seen in my life. Yet if it helps you to believe in him, then I'll just have to try to accept it. But I don't want to see you get hurt."

"I won't get hurt, Mom. Jesus doesn't hurt. He heals."

"I'm glad you believe that, Beverly. Having hope is so important in a life as difficult as yours. If you have found a way to have faith and friends who care about you, I am very happy for you. I love you and want only the best for you. We can agree to disagree and not be disagreeable, right?"

"Right, Mom. Thanks." I wipe the tears from my eyes.

"Now, about your book . . . Did you have to mention the cockroaches? Couldn't you have just said that Grandma's apartment wasn't quite as neat as it could have been? . . ."

I am aroused from my reverie by the sight of a large sign: SMALL ANIMAL HOSPITAL. I bring the car to a stop in front of the entrance. Entering the single story building, I announce my presence at the desk.

A young veterinary student approaches me. Her face is sullen as she hesitantly tells me that it doesn't look good for Jennifer. "We expected her to be doing much better by now, although she is an older dog and may need more time to recover from the surgery."

"Is she suffering?" I ask, tears beginning to flow as I think of possibly having to put Jennifer to sleep.

"Well, we have her on a lot of medication, so I think she's comfortable."

I am not comforted. She looked horrible yesterday as she lay pros-
trate on the cage floor, panting heavily. I could barely stand the pain of
that sight.

"Would you like to see her?"

I nod with trepidation.

Motioning me to follow her, the student offers, "I'll go with you
to the ICU. I haven't seen her since early this morning."

As I nervously walk down the corridor, I think of all the prayers
that were raised to the Lord in church this morning on behalf of my
ailing companion. Will our petitions be granted?

We make our way into the ICU. The dreaded antiseptic odor
assaults my nose. The cages, stacked one upon another, shelter quiver-
ing, suffering animals. I stare at the ground to spare myself the agony
of the sight. Out of the corner of my eye, I see a black-and-white dog
sitting up in her cage . . . almost perky. I do a double take. Could that
possibly be Jennifer? As I approach the kennel, I stare at the dog in
amazement. Jennifer has miraculously come to life.

The student fumbles for words. "Well . . . um . . . she was not like
that when I saw her this morning. I don't know what happened."

I do.

I take Jennifer home the following day and watch with delight as
she romps around the apartment, ecstatic to be reunited with family
and home. I am filled with a sense of awe. Her recovery is truly a
miracle from God.

As I reflect upon the momentous events of the last few days, I am
struck by a stunning revelation. My words from the pulpit yesterday
were my testimony to a living God. And his works are his living testimony to me.

15

. . . AND GRACE WILL
Lead Me Home

January 31, 1999

"Amazing grace! how sweet . . ."

The sound of three hundred voices echoes throughout the sanctuary as the old, familiar hymn is raised to the Lord. I struggle to stand, leaning on my cane for support as I attempt to balance the hymnal with my left hand. No effort is too great a struggle when praising the Lord. My spirit soars as I propel the stirring verses skyward:

> "I once was lost but now I'm found,
> Was blind but now I see."

A well-wisher finds me in the back row and gently pats me on the shoulder as he makes his way to his seat. I nod appreciatively. I am so grateful for the outpouring of love I have received from this embracing congregation. Strengthened by the support of the devoted worshipers who surround me, my voice grows louder and more passionate:

> "How precious did that grace appear
> The hour I first believed."

How my life has changed since becoming a believer. Not that I have been physically healed. Yet while I continue to suffer from illness, no longer do I suffer. For I have discovered that true suffering is separation from the Lord. I may be physically broken, but I am spiritually whole. The passionate voices fill my soul, revitalizing my weary body:

"He will my shield and portion be,
As long as life endures."

As the refrains cease, Pastor Dave asks that we be seated. "Today we have a special privilege. Our speaker, Anatoly, is the pastor of our sister church in Russia, where we have sent Pastor Harold on several occasions to help set up a recovery ministry. To assist Anatoly, we have provided him with a volunteer from right here in town who will attempt to interpret. Interestingly, he happens to be Jewish. Anatoly, we look forward to hearing you give us the Word of God."

A good-looking young man with blue eyes, dark hair, and rosy cheeks rises to stand before the congregation. He grins shyly as he is warmly welcomed with applause. I eye him with piqued curiosity. Such classic Russian features, a gentle face, a pleasant smile. As he begins to speak, the Jewish translator attempts to decipher his words: "I welcome you with the love of our dear Jesus Christ. . . ."

The interpreter hesitates then halts, looking over at the preacher with questioning eyes to elicit feedback regarding the accuracy of his translation. He is apparently at a disadvantage. Not only is the task of translating unfamiliar, but so is the vocabulary of the gospel. He continues interpreting, "I thank God for how he brought me and my brother here. I thank God that we're all one big family. God in his wonderful way was leading us to each other."

The struggling translator, standing next to this Russian pastor is, indeed, a strange sight. What is a Jew doing here laboring to communicate the gospel in the midst of all these Christians? I wonder who is truly the foreigner, the Russian pastor or the Jewish interpreter.

"And now I praise the Lord for he is great, and . . . I praise the Lord that Harold came to our church and found the language to communicate . . ." the translator continues.

Is this young Jew understanding the message he is delivering as he speaks the very words that, years ago, were used to coerce Jews in Russia and elsewhere into believing in Christianity or face continued persecution . . . or worse? I shake my head and try to erase such thoughts from my mind. The pogroms that killed my ancestors happened such a long time ago. We have come so very far since then, haven't we? I feel the haunting tug of my Jewish identity . . . and wonder where my loyalties lie. I glance around the sanctuary at the faces of the congregants, who are attempting to absorb the stirring words of the spirited pastor. My mind blurs as I stare at the countenance of this young Russian . . .

His eyes grow stone cold . . . He becomes frozen in time . . .

"Down with the Jews! Down with the Jews!" angry mobs scream as doors splinter and windows shatter somewhere beyond the pale. The brazen intruders descend upon the town, swinging clubs and swords, battering and piercing their defenseless victims. The thundering gallop of hooves punctuates the cries of bloodily beaten bodies. The murdered lie silent in the mud. The mob bludgeons and mutilates the corpses, attempting to

further torture victims who can no longer suffer.
Immense clouds of pillow feathers rise in the air as trea-
sured possessions are strewn into the street and trampled
amid the bodies. The young, blue-eyed pastor is seated
upon a horse, leading the death squad. I close my eyes
and brace for the attack.

"I thank God we're all one big family, and I'm really happy to see you today." Anatoly smiles. The Jewish translator wipes his brow nervously as his anxious eyes scan the crowd for their reaction.

I can't believe my ears. The incongruous words assault me with their irony.

"What?" I speak to the sword-bearing, sweet-talk-
ing hypocrite who has invaded my mind. "Your people
killed almost every one of my maternal relatives in the
pogroms in the early 1900s. Only my grandmother and
grandfather escaped death by fleeing to America. My
uncle joined them shortly thereafter but returned home-
sick to his beloved Russian homeland, where he was bru-
tally slaughtered along with thousands of innocent men,
women, and children—just because they were Jews. It
has even been said that seminary students were sent to
instigate pogroms in Jewish villages. And your church
stood silent!"

The pastor does not flinch as he continues to address the congregation. I turn away. What am I doing here in the midst of all these

Christians? Was my father right? Are all non-Jews anti-Semitic deep down inside? How could I have been so naive? I scrutinize my surroundings while trying to hide the hurt . . . and my tears. It's the same familiar church I entered for the first time as a follower of Christ. I remember falling to my knees, clutching the shiny golden cross on that communion table while proclaiming my love for Jesus. Weeping, I gave thanks to him for carrying me through so many interminable nights of illness and despair, and for resurrecting me with him to such lofty heights. That selfless rabbi, that precious Lord, who changed the world with his message of love and brotherhood, had rescued me.

> *Jesus, save me! I plead as tears flood my mind. The dreaded horses continue to gallop toward me, gaining speed, poised for attack. The Russian pastor reaches for his sword and aims it directly at me, ready to draw blood. Suddenly Jesus comes, alighting on the scarlet earth. Thundering steeds come to a grinding halt. Brawling mobs cease their plundering. Wounded victims miraculously heal. The dead rise. All is still. Not a whisper. Not a breath. In the profound silence, the anguished groans of the gentle, wounded warrior of peace tear at the soul—Jesus is weeping.*

The Russian pastor's expression softens. Compassion returns to the faces of the congregants. Anatoly continues to speak. "When I see today your beautiful children singing for God, I remember times when our teachers in Sunday school for teaching God's Word were put in jail. Women who were teaching children to love God, the peace of Christ.

It was very painful to be a Christian family for us . . . I was called an American spy because I was from a Christian family. But we don't hate people who denied and pushed away the church. Now we're happy that people are coming to church who used to be Communists, used to be members of the Communist Party.

"A few weeks ago I had a phone call. The old voice said hi to me. He said, 'You've probably heard about me. You have no idea the evil I brought to you, your family, your church. And I'm sick now, and I can't even walk. It worries me that I did that.' He asked me if I could forgive him. And I was really touched that this person called me. And I thought about Jesus Christ on the cross. Jesus looked at the people who crucified him and asked, 'Father, forgive them because they do not know what they are doing.' And I said to him that I'm happy from my heart, from the heart of my people, and from the people who were in jail because of him. I told him that I've forgiven him. He thanked me. And in two days I saw in the newspaper that he had died. And I believe he went in peace with God."

Anatoly's remarkable message astonishes me. This pastor of a Russian church, who only moments before seemed to me to be the living embodiment of centuries of anti-Semitism, had himself fallen victim to a common enemy—hatred. Yet he came here today to preach a message of love, brotherhood, and forgiveness.

I reflect upon this extraordinary scene. Here I am, an American Jew of Eastern European descent, sitting in a church filled with American Christians, watching a Russian-American Jewish translator attempt to communicate the words of a Russian pastor. Where would I find a more diverse and potentially contentious collection of human beings? Yet here we sit in love and peace because we reside in the presence of the Prince of Peace—Jesus Christ. In his light, differences are overshadowed by the commonalties that bind us together. We see in each other what we see in ourselves. And we do unto others as we would have them do unto us. Not one of us has been spared the disgrace of sin. Not one of us should fail to seek the grace of forgiveness.

The body of Christ, this precious living organism that embodies the spirit of the Lord, encompasses all who come with willing hearts from every age, gender, and ethnicity from all over the world. What an awesome thought that after centuries of misunderstanding, hatred, and violence perpetrated in the name of Jesus Christ, this Christian family can genuinely embrace me . . . and I can truly love them. And together, we can do good in his name.

After the service, I wait in line to greet Anatoly. As our eyes finally meet, we engage in a handshake that spans the generations. We go in peace.

The nippy January breeze greets me as I exit the church. High above, two sparrows launch themselves into the blustery wind from the safety of the steeple. They struggle to take flight but are tossed mercilessly by the unrelenting gales. Suddenly, as if supported by an invisible hand, they steady themselves and take wing, soaring to the heavens.

I brace myself for the journey ahead. All of a sudden, the wind ceases. The fluttering fringes of my scarf land gracefully upon my shoulders. My leg muscles, sore and weak from straining to gain momentum, relax. In the uncanny silence, I can almost hear a voice whisper, *Peace . . . be still.* A profound calm pervades my body and soul. In this blessed interlude, I find renewed reassurance. In the bitter circumstances I must bear, I will endure—in the warmth and safety of the boundless and abiding love of Jesus Christ.

The sweet verses of that stirring old hymn we shared together echo through my soul. I am truly amazed!

"Thro' many dangers, toils and snares,
I have already come;
'Tis grace hath brought me safe thus far,
And grace will lead me home."

Epilogue

Faith led me to write this book—faith that the Lord would carry me through the many difficulties I would face in undertaking a project of this magnitude while coping with a debilitating disease, and faith in the love and steadfast efforts of family and friends. That this book has been brought to completion is a testament to that faith. I now humbly release my words into the world and hope that my story will be an inspiration to many. For me, it is a great blessing to have this privilege. Through these many years of illness and isolation, I have come to know the haunting pain of a silenced voice.

When I began this project, I had feared that I would have to leave the reader steeped in medical mystery. Certainly, after so many years of searching for a diagnosis, I did not expect a definitive answer to suddenly materialize at the completion of this book. But I had underestimated the power of the Lord and the generosity of the human heart. For, during the writing of this manuscript, I met the Muscular Dystrophy Association researcher who discovered the key to my illness. This world-renowned scientist epitomizes humility, for he chooses to remain anonymous, asking instead that his entire research team be credited with successfully arriving at a diagnosis. Yet he deserves credit far beyond his scientific accomplishments, for he took a moment out of his extremely busy schedule to compassionately listen to my story. And despite his immense obligations that take him around the world, he offered me his help. That act of kindness and generosity eventually led to the answer . . . and changed my life.

The results of his recent analysis of my muscle biopsy sample from 1992 were mentioned earlier in this book. This data, which was preliminary and tentative due to the age and miniscule size of the sample, pointed toward mitochondrial myopathy (neuromuscular disease).

Recently, upon his recommendation, I underwent a second muscle biopsy—an open surgical procedure. A larger sample was extracted from my left quadriceps muscle and flown to his lab. His analysis confirmed the diagnosis of mitochondrial myopathy characterized by a severe cytochrome c oxidase (COX) deficiency. He also found deficiencies in other enzymes and biochemical compounds, prompting further investigation. In addition, cutting-edge genetic testing on my tissue will continue into the future. If a specific defect in my genes can be found, doctors may someday be able to correct the mutation with gene therapy. For now, this dedicated researcher is closely monitoring my case, searching for ways to slow or reverse the disease process. His tireless efforts are very encouraging, particularly since my disease has progressed to mitochondrial encephalomyopathy. This means that not only are my muscles affected but also parts of my brain. The result is that I am having increasing difficulty with motor control. The lack of coordination that began in my hands has now progressed to my legs.

The gift I have been given by this caring researcher cannot be measured. It is the precious gift of hope.

My wish is that this crucial research will receive generous donations so that countless children and adults afflicted with mitochondrial disease might someday be freed of their suffering. If you wish to be a part of the cure, you may send your tax-free donation check (memo line: For mitochondrial disease research) to:

Columbia University
Health Sciences Development Office
Department of Neurology
100 Haven Ave., Suite 29D
New York, NY 10032
212-304-7200

I pray that all who seek will find comfort, hope, and renewal in the pages of this book. If the trials of my life and the amazing answers I have gained can touch another searching soul, I am deeply grateful and profoundly humbled.

I have come to realize that it was not my illness that grounded me. We are all caterpillars dreaming of flight. My disability was merely the chrysalis through which my soul could be transformed so that it might take wing.

In the presence of God, I look upon my life on this earth with new perspective and appreciation. I view each God-given moment as a golden opportunity to honor the Lord and elevate my life by choosing to do good. I have discovered that, despite my physical limitations, I can turn ordinary moments into extraordinary moments by reaching out to others with a knowing smile, a kind word, a loving presence. Even these seemingly small acts of kindness can transform the mundane moments of life into special opportunities to impact lives in a way far beyond what we can imagine or will ever know. And, perhaps, what is most amazing is that we who give are the ones who are most blessed.

It is my greatest wish that all human beings follow the example of Jesus by embracing all creatures great and small with love and compassion.

Above all, may those who profess to follow Jesus Christ do only *good* in His name.

ACKNOWLEDGMENTS

I wish to express my gratitude to Patti Stadolnik, a cherished friend whose contributions have extended far beyond her valuable editorial assistance and technical support. She has been a daily inspiration and driving force in bringing this project to fruition. Patti's grace and gentle nature made possible an open personal and theological dialogue that significantly shaped this book. In the process, she enabled me to find the best in myself. I could not have asked for a better partner. She was a godsend. Patti, although I know you are tired of hearing me say this, I am eternally grateful to you . . . and for you.

I would also like to express my appreciation to Patti's family—her husband, Rob, and children, Mark, Joseph, and Laura—for patiently enduring the inconvenience of having a wife and mom immersed for so many hours in such an all-consuming project.

There is no way to adequately express my appreciation to Kathy Helmers of Alive Communications, Inc. for taking this first-time author under her wing so that her dreams could take flight. Thank you, Kathy, for your invaluable guidance, steadfast support, and enthusiastic encouragement. You've changed my life.

To Alice Crider, Kathy's outstanding assistant, whose competence is only exceeded by the depth of her compassion, thanks for so graciously helping me to navigate through uncharted waters.

To Byron Williamson, Joey Paul, and the staff at Integrity Publishers, Inc., thank you for the privilege of working with you.

I am also grateful to Sue Ann Jones for being so gracious and supportive during the editorial phase of this book.

My brother, Ed, is introduced in the pages of this book. It never ceases to amaze me how his brotherly love, support, and generosity have continued to grow throughout the years. I had feared that my inclusion of his memorable childhood antics would be a source of some embarrassment to him. But such is his giving heart that he allowed me to enhance my book with these stories. I am so grateful for the many hours he spent working on this project. While he remains committed to his faith, he understands and supports my decision to follow Jesus. He says he will never join me. Whether or not he does, we will continue to walk the earth with the deepest love and respect for one another. He has said there is nothing he wouldn't do for me. Ditto, Ed.

I am also deeply grateful to my father for his loving support and encouragement throughout the writing of this book. Even though he has not been in the best of health, he has read my manuscript five times. He even requested that a copy be brought to him during his recent hospital stay. Such is the great love of my father that he would make this effort in the midst of serious medical struggles. He says that this book has enabled him to more fully understand my belief in Jesus. I am so grateful for his open-mindedness . . . and for his not losing faith in me because of my newfound faith. Dad, I love you very much. Thanks for everything.

To Pat, who has consistently supported my efforts and encouraged me to believe that "you can always do something to make it better," thank you from the bottom of my heart. You were right.

Spiritual encouragement comes from knowing those who walk with the Lord in their hearts. I have been most fortunate to befriend a "pastor of hearts," Rev. Dave Stewart. He is that rare individual whose sensitivity and compassion draw others to him and draw him to those who suffer. He is a faithful companion of the sick and hurting, keeping vigil with them in their darkest hours. In him I see the living example of a true Christian heart. Dave, I thank the Lord for your presence in my life.

Many loving friends have supported me through prayer, daily encouragement, and numerous acts of kindness. I would like to thank a few of them here: Pat Ahern, Lily and Edmond Barschak, Betty Carter, Lynn Duquette, Lorraine Forman, Mario and Becky Gabrielli, Carol Goldman, Gail Harlin, Keri Patterson, Lynne and David Redonnet, Cindy Stewart, and Anne Weber.

To those too numerous to acknowledge by name, I extend my heartfelt gratitude for your generosity and support. May you all be richly and forever blessed.